LOREE BOHL

Withdrawn

FEARLESS GARDENING

Be
Bold

Break
the
Rules

Grow
What
You
Love

LOREE BOHL

FEARLESS GARDENING

Be
Bold

Break
the
Rules

Grow
What
You
Love

Frontispiece: A blooming cactus (likely *Opuntia* 'Santa Rita') and *Euphorbia rigida*, flourishing not in the desert Southwest, but at McMenamins Kennedy School in Portland, Oregon.

The Haseltine Building
133 S.W. Second Avenue, Suite 450
Portland, Oregon 97204-3527
timberpress.com

Printed in China
Book design by Vincent James
ISBN 978-1-60469-962-3

A catalog record for this book is available from the
Library of Congress and the British Library.

To every gardener
who has ever thought,
but I can't or I shouldn't,
yes you can and
yes you should.

CONTENTS

INTRODUCTION

I want to inspire you to look at plants differently and see your garden through new eyes—to treat gardening as an adventure, to embrace the freedom to explore a new type of plant, and then to plant it just because you want to. Why not surround yourself with plants you love? Who cares if they're not supposed to be planted together, might eventually crowd each other, or aren't everyone's cup of tea? It's your garden and you should love it; you should be having fun.

Gardening is an opportunity to create something completely personal and to see your dream become a reality. At its most inspiring, I find gardening to be a series of experiments: exciting, challenging, and sometimes surprising experiments. Although it shouldn't be the case, many gardeners need permission to try things and make mistakes. By the power vested in me as the author of this book, I hereby grant you that permission. Gardening is not a straight line. There are many detours along the way, and thankfully, you never actually arrive at the finish. Gardening is my passion; I hope it is or will be yours, too.

> "People think about the word 'fearless' to mean 'without fear,' but I see it to actually mean with fear but you did it anyway."
>
> —Luvvie Ajayi, writer, activist, self-proclaimed professional troublemaker

After gardening in containers and on windowsills for years, I finally became a home and garden owner. It was time to plant, but I couldn't decide where. I circled my front yard with two tiny bare-root peonies in my hands, searching for the perfect spot to plant them. Obviously, a decision so significant could not be made lightly. I considered what seemed to be all the important things, like how I would move through the garden, the color of the flowers, and how often I would see them and smell their seductive scent. I thought about what I wanted my garden to say about me to the neighborhood. I may have given the peonies' light requirements and their eventual size a passing thought, but I wouldn't bet on it. I finally planted them. Then I realized I had made a horrible mistake, dug them up, and replanted them in what seemed like a better spot. I ended up moving those damned peonies so many times that I finally killed one of them. The remaining one found a home in a perfectly picturesque spot near the living room window—right in front of the hose bib. I was unfamiliar with the devastation an unruly rubber hose could wreak on a plant.

I'd like to say the fear and uncertainty that gripped me that day was a one-time thing, but I felt it again and again as I made my first garden. Gardening is serious business, I thought at the time, and sometimes still do. As with all things serious, I knew there were rules—Gardening Commandments, the right way to do it. Doing it wrong would have serious consequences. It's perfectly natural to fear doing something wrong, to make mistakes. Plus, plants are scary; they're living things with needs. Who wants to fail dramatically in front of the neighbors, with dead plants and wasted money?

"Given the fact that the most spectacular gardeners are the ones that fail the most spectacularly, it's really critical to get over your fear of failure. It's an indication of your adventurousness. So many home gardeners are afraid of the failure because they are disempowered when in fact there's no other way to learn other than to laugh at your failures and try again . . . Good gardening is not about knowing it all and guaranteed success; it's about accepting the mystery and ambiguity of the process."

—Michael McCoy, in *The Planthunter* online

I developed an obsession with the desert Southwest on a long-ago business trip to Arizona. The plants and gardens there were unlike anything I'd seen before, so different from those back home in the Pacific Northwest. I was particularly taken with agaves; they were unbelievable—like spiky sculptures come to life. I wanted to surround myself with them and began growing a few small ones in containers when I returned home. They vacationed on my patio in Spokane, Washington, during the summer and I brought them back inside the house for winter. I was happy with this arrangement.

Shortly after moving to Portland, Oregon, everything changed. People who don't live here think it rains all the time, and truth be told we can grow a mean patch of moss without even trying. Imagine my surprise when I spotted a large *Agave parryi*—an agave, the plant of the desert—growing in the ground here in Portland. It was actually growing in a pocket of a rock wall, but all I saw was an agave in the ground. Rain be damned—I had moved to a place where I could finally plant these sculptural beauties in the ground! At that moment, I saw my future garden and knew there would be agaves, a lot of them.

A year later, when I finally had a garden, I bought an agave and put it in the ground. I was thrilled—then winter came. That poor agave rotted and became a pile of dead, stinky mush. This could have been the end of my agave dreams, but I was not willing to give up. I tried again and again, and eventually, I hit upon the right combination of species, a good location, and adequate soil prepa-ration. Now several agaves are thriving in my garden. I did it poorly until I did it well. I made mistakes and I learned from them. That's when I began to garden fearlessly—or, as Luvvie Ajayi would say, with fear, but I did it anyway.

My garden will never be finished. I'm constantly learning about plants, about gardening in my climate, and about design, so what I want from my garden changes. I gardened for two years at my first home and barely scratched the surface of what I wanted that garden to be. I've lived in my current home for more than a decade and I've planted trees that have almost grown to maturity. I've witnessed several of my plants die from harsh winters. I've torn out and redesigned entire sections of the garden that originally thrilled me, then became boring and prompted me to try for something better. I keep learning, and I continue to expand what my garden can be.

I begin this book with an introduction to a pair of women who created exceptional gardens and whose approach to doing so inspires me. Then I share a few Gardening Commandments you may have heard—ideas that at first intimidated me, but over the years I've retooled to suit my style and needs. I encourage you to do the same. The next section looks at how to go about creating a garden you'll love: defining what it means for a garden to be "in good taste" and acknowledging that plants are going to die—and that sometimes that's a good thing. I'll introduce you to "cramscaping," one of my favorite terms, and share tips that will help you identify your own style.

Gardening is full of opportunities to play and experiment, and there is an entire chapter devoted to doing just that: stumperies, vertical gardening, crevice gardens, and more . . . oh, the possibilities! Containers expand what we can grow and are a go-to strategy in my garden. I share numerous examples of how you can employ them to boost your garden's potential.

Because people who garden "outside the lines" seem naturally drawn to the unexpected, we'll take a look at what that means in the landscape; I'll also suggest some best practices for doing it successfully. In addition, I share some plants that I love and think you might too. The final chapter takes an in-depth look at seven rule-breaking gardens, or collections of gardens, and the people who have created and tend them.

Even though I'm going to do my best to push a few of my favorite plants on you, what you won't find are lengthy plant lists with specific cultural requirements for long-term plant happiness. That's not to say such information isn't important—it's the most important element for healthy plants and a thriving garden—but since all gardening is local, you'd be best suited to research your own growing conditions. Please find books on this topic and read them. Talk to your local nurseries and plant stores, and with gardeners in your neighborhood and online—these are valuable resources.

A note about location. I'm firmly planted in Portland, Oregon. Many of the gardens I write about are here in the Pacific Northwest. However, it is possible to live anywhere and be a fearless gardener. Location shouldn't determine, or limit, your attitude and approach to gardening. There are times—many times—I wish I lived in Santa Barbara, California, where I would be able to take advantage of the mild climate found there. But since I don't, I garden like I do, in the ways that I can. The principles of fearless gardening apply no matter where you call home.

It's my hope that new and seasoned gardeners alike will discover things that will interest and inspire them in these pages. After all, every gardener is a beginner at something. I'm reminded of a conversation I had with a man who was selling off a significant plant collection, along with his home and greenhouse, as he was preparing to move into a retirement facility. He didn't grieve over the aging of his body but over the inability to plant new things and see them mature. He had just discovered and was captivated by *Magnolia macrophylla*, a new-to-him tree that he wanted to grow. This fellow had spent a lifetime traveling, collecting plants, and learning about them; he wanted to keep doing so. Gardeners are always learning, experimenting, and trying new things.

Clockwise from top:

An eclectic mix of plants, including many not expected outside a desert climate, thrive in my Pacific Northwest garden.

Podophyllum peltatum emerges from a sea of *Adiantum venustum*; the large striped bromeliad is *Vriesea fosteriana* 'Red Chestnut'.

Agave parryi 'J.C. Raulston' in my Portland, Oregon, garden. After a few ill-fated attempts to get agaves established, I finally succeeded. Now, even the occasional ice storm doesn't faze them.

THERE IS
NO RIGHT WAY
TO GARDEN

While making my second garden, I learned about two women who have since become my gardening mentors, if only in spirit: Ruth Bancroft and Ganna Walska. Their individual approaches to the art of gardening could not have been more different, yet they both inspire me with their "I'll do it my way, thank you" attitude and their limitless passion for what they were creating. Both had extremely personal visions of what they wanted their gardens to become and stopped at nothing to see that vision through to reality. They created captivating, one-of-a-kind, private gardens that are now open to the public.

Ruth and Ganna both lived to advanced ages: Ruth to 109 and Ganna to 96. I want to believe their strong wills and time spent working in their gardens contributed to their longevity. I was fortunate to meet Ruth Bancroft before her death in 2017, but Ganna passed away in 1984, long before I began gardening.

Ruth Bancroft and Her Groundbreaking Dry Garden

Ruth Bancroft created what is now known as the Ruth Bancroft Garden in Walnut Creek, California. She was enamored with cactus and succulents before they were popular, or even widely available. Ruth researched, made lists, and acquired plants primarily via travel to Southern California nurseries. As her containerized collection grew, Ruth began to experiment with planting in the ground around her home, observing and learning as she went. When plants died, she examined them for clues to their demise. When she discovered rotten roots were the culprit, she set about creating raised planting berms for increased drainage.

At the age of 63—after her hard-sought collection began to outgrow the structures built to contain it—Ruth's husband encouraged her to plant their recently cleared orchard. The year was 1971 and the Ruth Bancroft Garden was born. Today the garden is a showplace for growing cactus and succulents and has become a model for dry gardening (using little to no supplemental water). Ruth was a self-taught gardener for whom thrift was a guiding principle. Most of the plants in the garden started out in small four- or six-inch containers, occasionally a gallon-sized pot. Ruth claimed to be a collector, not a designer, so she hired Lester Hawkins—a

Previous: *Aloe striata* (coral aloe) blooms in the eclectic Ruth Bancroft Garden in Walnut Creek, California.

Ruth Bancroft, enjoying her remarkable garden in 1992.

Clockwise from top left:

A patch of blue *Senecio serpens* is backed by a purple-tinged *Aloe capitata* var. *quartziticola* hybrid and a blooming *Aloe arborescens*, at the Ruth Bancroft Garden.

Agave ovatifolia 'Vanzie', a cultivar of whale's tongue agave, is hard to miss.

Plants under the shade structure at the Ruth Bancroft Garden include (left to right) a variegated *Agave americana*, *Aloe africana* (blooming), *Agave attentuata*, *Espostoa melanostele*, and *Aloe vanbalenii* (blooming). The structure is enclosed in the winter for added protection from the cold.

well-known designer and nurseryman—to assist with the overall layout of the garden. The work of planting out the garden was all hers, however.

In Johanna Silver's book *The Bold Dry Garden: Lessons from the Ruth Bancroft Garden*, Ruth describes pushing the edge of expected plant hardiness in her garden, planting things that weren't thought to grow in her area of California. "I've tried a number of them, and some do all right, and some don't. But I always like to try something, if I like the plant itself. See how it will do." How do you know if you don't try? Ruth was a fearless gardener, blazing her own trail and educating others as she went.

WHAT I LEARNED FROM RUTH:

- You're never too old to start a garden.
- Garden as though you will live forever—you just might live to 109.
- Embrace the idiosyncrasies of your site.
- Acquire plants that thrill you, even if they aren't in fashion.
- It's okay to start small; plants grow and you don't have to pay for instant impact.
- Believe in your vision even if no one else is gardening the way you want to. Share your hard-earned knowledge with others.
- Don't let the death of a plant keep you from trying it again. Investigate and learn from what went wrong—experiment.

Ganna Walska: Self-Proclaimed "Enemy of the Average"

While I like to muse on Ruth and Ganna walking in each other's gardens and sharing stories about their favorite plants, I can't find any record of them meeting and I don't know that they would have enjoyed each other's company if they had. While Ruth valued practicality, Ganna was an over-the-top, more-is-better personality.

Born Hanna Puacz in Poland in 1887, Ganna Walska changed her name for a life on the stage. Her career as an opera singer allowed her to travel the world and assume the glamorous life-style of a socialite. Ganna collected many things, including jewelry and husbands—the plants came later. In her autobiography, *Always Room at the Top*, Ganna famously declared herself to be an "enemy of the average."

After visiting Santa Barbara, California, in 1941, Ganna and her sixth—and last—husband purchased the 37-acre Montecito estate that would become the garden paradise known as Lotusland. As a visitor to Lotusland, you quickly realize nothing was too much for Madame Walska: rare plants, huge specimens, mass plantings of a single species, and entire collections acquired and planted in the garden together. In Ganna's world, if something was worth doing, it was worth doing in a big way. If one was good, three would be better, and five were preferred.

Legend has it that when Ganna spotted a plant she wanted while motoring around Santa Barbara, she would dispatch her chauffeur to make an offer, even sending champagne, until the object of her affection became hers. When she needed money to complete the cycad garden at Lotusland, she financed the work by

Ganna Walska poses with a kniphofia in bloom at Lotusland, circa 1955.

Top: *Echinocactus grusonii* (golden barrel cactus) is planted en masse around the main house at Lotusland.

Bottom: Ganna sold pieces of her jewelry to raise funds to finish the Cycad Garden at Lotusland.

auctioning off some of her jewelry collection. Where Ganna had the will, there was always a way.

On our first visit to Lotusland, my husband feared the garden would be a jumble of plants, thrown together haphazardly with shells and garden art, all competing for attention. He was pleased to be wrong. Ganna was a gifted designer—often contradicting those she hired to help create the gardens, while managing to make the biggest and best plants work together harmoniously.

WHAT I LEARNED FROM GANNA:

- Go big—your imagination is the only limitation to what your garden can be.

- A cohesive garden can be built from plant collections.

- Consult experts, but stay true to your dream.

- One person's kitsch is another's perfect garden accessory. Giant clamshells as fountains and abalone shells as garden décor? Why not?

- Don't be afraid to knock on doors and ask homeowners about plants—most gardeners are happy to share a cutting or seeds (champagne usually not required).

Ganna Walska: Self-Proclaimed "Enemy of the Average"

What would Ruth and Ganna do?

Shortly after I completed the planting of my front garden, several neighbors good-naturedly commented that "it's going to look great when things grow a bit," as though I needed encouragement to not be underwhelmed with what I'd created. That's when I realized I was seeing the tiny plantings as what they would become, rather than what they were. I was wearing my "garden future" glasses, à la Ruth Bancroft. A few years later, after the garden had filled in, another neighbor shared that she finally understood what I'd done. She had been confused by the lack of lawn and thought I'd gone a little overboard with the number of plants—as if that was possible! My inner Ganna was thrilled: too many plants sounded just about right. Gardening for yourself is wonderful, but it's even better when others appreciate it too.

Like Ruth and Ganna, gardening is in my blood. Researching new plants, tracking them down, and watching them grow satisfies my desire to learn. Anyone who has bought a plant knows that moment of wonder: "What will this fantastic green thing I'm holding in my hands become?" When my tiny garden plants went in, I felt like I had dozens of interesting experiments happening just outside my front door. "When will the bark on the *Arctostaphylos* × 'Austin Griffiths' start to peel?" and "Is that what *Callistemon viridiflorus* buds look like?" I wondered. I was so excited when my *Agave parryi* 'J.C. Raulston' sent out a pup. Walking the garden daily was exhilarating.

A garden is a natural outlet for design energy: from planning the layout, to matching a new plant with its perfect container, to exploring plant combinations and coming up with creative ways to work in more plants. In fact, gardening doesn't just provide

Giant clamshell fountains and the abalone shell pond are part of Lotusland's Aloe Garden.

numerous opportunities to be creative, it actually allows us to think more creatively in every aspect of our lives. I'm reminded of something I read while visiting the Amazon Spheres, three glass-domed conservatories at the headquarters campus of Amazon, in Seattle, Washington: "Imagine a work conversation happening near a waterfall or a flowering wall of orchids. Even short doses of nature have been proven to boost well-being. Immersed in greenery, we're more relaxed and alert—we can think more creatively." Relaxed and alert—that seems like a contradiction, doesn't it? But those somewhat opposing states of being describe perfectly how I feel when I'm in the flow in my garden: energized, focused, yet relaxed and enjoying the task at hand.

Control, and the complete lack thereof, is another gardening paradox. As we design plantings and decide what the overall look and feel of the garden will be, we're in control. However, as soon as we plant and step away, we've given up that control and nature takes over; that's when strange and wonderful, sometimes unfortunate, things happen. As gardeners, we learn to let go and later how to step back in and reclaim control—prune, remove, redesign—and then give up control again.

Gardeners can't help but feel calm and connected when gardening. Digging in the soil, weeding, spreading compost, these things calm us. It's busywork—busy *hands* work—and many researchers believe that working with our hands grounds us while also engaging our brain in a way that just makes us feel better. Garden work is anticomputer. When our fingers spend an hour hitting buttons on the keyboard, we tend to feel a little tense, whereas an hour spent in the garden, doing even the most mundane task, relaxes us. The connection gardening provides to the larger world cannot be overstated. Gardening matters, gardening connects us, and, as Ruth and Ganna knew, there is a lot of joy to be found in sharing this passion.

About Those Gardening Commandments

Anytime I leaf through a magazine and come across titles like "Ten Things to Do Now in the Garden," "Five Plants You Should Be Growing," or "Thirty Ways to Leave Your Laurel," I hear an editor telling a writer, "Make me a list, I need a list!" I call these garden rules, handed down by so-called experts, the Gardening Commandments. Gardens aren't "one size fits all." There is no single way to approach making a garden.

When I was a beginning gardener, I thought I had to follow the Gardening Commandments. If this is what the experts believe, who was I to question it? Now I recognize that gardens are individual creations. What works in one may not work in another. How many times have you heard that you shouldn't rake leaves in autumn? Leave them in your garden, "they" say, to naturally decompose and feed the soil—sometimes you're told to mow the leaves into smaller bits, but not always. That advice might work with small leaves like a honey locust, but imagine leaving the two-foot leaves of *Magnolia macrophylla* in place, or even trying to mow them smaller.

What about leaves on gravel? What's the point of decorative gravel mulch if you let it become covered in decomposing leaves? Plus, it's risky to let winter-wet leaves accumulate around the base of hardy succulents like agaves, where they block air circulation and can lead to rot. While decomposed leaves can add valuable organic material to the soil, it's also okay to rake and compost them. You aren't a bad gardener if you choose to get rid of your leaves. Don't let anyone tell you otherwise!

Rather than following the Gardening Commandments without question, I encourage you to consider the knowledge on

Just a few of the many *Magnolia macrophylla* leaves that fall from my tree each autumn. Can you imagine leaving these to decompose in place?

which they're based, then evaluate that information by filtering it through your own personal experience and garden conditions. Decide which rules you want to follow, and which ones you want to bend or break. No one knows your site or your garden desires like you. Remember that many of these ideas aren't hard facts; they're simply popular opinions. The following are a few of the Gardening Commandments I've questioned and then approached in my own way. How will you rewrite them for your garden?

Commandment 1: Thou shalt plan the entire garden before you begin planting.

When starting a new garden, it makes sense to loosely map out where major features such as a patio, vegetable garden, cutting garden, storage, seating, or pathways will go before you jump in and start planting. This might be a sketch you come up with on your own or something you put together with the help of a friend whose style you admire. Maybe you decide to work with a professional designer; many are willing to do a basic garden consultation for a reasonable fee.

But don't feel like you have to wait for the pathway and patio locations to be finalized or installed before you head to your favorite nursery and indulge in a little plant-purchasing therapy. Sometimes looking at nothing but the big picture can be overwhelming and even demoralizing.

My peony planting and the resulting paralysis was part of beginning to claim an existing garden as my own. By adding a few plants every chance I got, the space slowly transformed into my garden. My meager budget did not include funds for big changes. Looking at the garden I had, and comparing it to the garden I wanted, could easily have become an exercise in losing hope. However, by jumping in and getting started, I was taking charge in the only way I could. Doing so gave me a path forward. I started small and built out from there, gradually adopting a fearless attitude as I went.

Ruth Bancroft approached each planting island as a separate garden all its own. That same approach can be used no matter the size of your plot. If you're unsure of exactly where to begin, I suggest choosing a planting area that's easily accessible and visible from multiple locations, one that will give you the most impact. Start small. By concentrating your initial efforts in a smaller space, you'll set yourself up for success. Buying enough plants to fill a 5000-square-foot lot is prohibitively expensive and, unless you purchase by the truckload, they'll disappear once planted. In contrast, by focusing on a smaller area, your plants will wow you with their impact. After you've created one small oasis, you'll be ready to tackle the next spot, and the next.

Commandment 2: Thou shalt not purchase plants on impulse.

Those in the know say you should research plants before heading to the nursery and always shop from a list, but that's just crazy talk. People who shop and garden like that probably only wear practical shoes and never have a glass of wine with lunch (ahem, not that there's anything wrong with either of those choices). I understand the reasoning behind the rule. Its advocates want to make sure you have both the space in your garden for the plant's eventual size, and that the conditions found in your garden are a match for the plant's cultural needs. Both are important factors when shopping for a plant you want to become a cornerstone of the garden—a shade tree, for example. However, not every plant needs to be a lifetime commitment.

I'm a firm believer in supporting locally owned nurseries, but I do occasionally stroll through the garden center at a big-box store. On one such outing, I came upon a deeply discounted chocolate mimosa, *Albizia julibrissin* 'Summer Chocolate'. I'd admired that tree for years in other people's gardens and at nurseries, but it was always priced a little too high for my budget, and I didn't have room in my garden for another tree. But there it was, tempting me with its dark, lacy foliage and an unbelievable price. What was a plant-lusting girl to do? Even though I didn't have a place for it in my garden, I bought it. It lived in a container for a couple of years until the perfect garden spot opened up. I am so glad I didn't talk myself out of it. Some impulse buys can become treasured garden features.

I'm here to tell you it's okay to buy a plant just because you love it, even if it's not a long-term match for your garden. Enjoy it, and let it go when it doesn't make you happy any longer. You appreciate cut flowers, don't you?

Not everyone would see room for another tree in this already full garden, but I managed to find a spot for an *Albizia julibrissin* 'Summer Chocolate'.

Commandment 3: **Thou shalt embrace fall planting.**

When I first heard "fall is for planting," I thought it had to be a slogan designed by the nursery industry to move their leftover inventory before winter arrived. A bit cynical? Yes. The truth is, there is good intent behind the push to plant in the fall—especially in a winter-wet/summer-dry climate, where rain helps roots become established before the following year's summer drought. The soil is still warm in the fall and roots are actively growing; an established root system will be better able to pull moisture from deep within the ground when water is limited. For these reasons, fall planting makes great sense when it comes to hardy trees or shrubs, or even perennials capable of tolerating temperatures much colder

Top: No lawn! Low-water plantings create a lively landscape in Tamara Paulat's Saint Helens, Oregon, garden.

Bottom: Vegetables in a pair of stock tank planters look right at home in a Portland front yard.

than what your area experiences in a typical winter. However, if you're planting a dry-loving succulent or a plant that's marginally hardy in your area, then in my experience you're setting yourself up for failure by planting in the fall. The plant will not have time to become established before winter sets in, with all the challenges that entails. In my garden, I maintain a cutoff date of June—early July at the latest—for planting hardy succulents like agave and cactus in the ground. Any later and the plants won't become sufficiently established to withstand winter conditions in my zone 8 garden. In addition to establishing roots, these plants need summer's heat to harden up. Trust me, I've planted later and have the dead plants on my conscience to prove it.

Commandment 4: Thou shalt keep thy front yard for lawn and thy backyard for thy garden.

The space we have available for gardening is shrinking; homes are getting larger and residential lots are getting smaller. Often a front yard is the sunniest patch of soil available. Why waste it on a lawn? Thankfully, lawn as the default approach to front yard design is becoming outdated, but not too long ago, homeowners were harassed for not conforming to the standard of the great American lawn. Folks with Home Owners Association rules may face some limitations on what they're able to plant, but people are breaking down those barriers as well.

In my part of the world, many residents allow their lawns to go dormant in the summer in the name of water conservation, knowing they will green up again when the rain returns in the fall. While I applaud the idea of not wasting water on a lawn, the reality is rather unpleasant. Who enjoys walking across crispy brown grass? Not to mention that there's just no way to make a dormant

About Those Gardening Commandments

lawn—and its accompanying weeds that refuse to go dormant—look inviting. I believe low-water plantings are a more attractive choice. Not only are they easier on the eyes, they add life to a space—not just plants, but birds and bees.

Thanks to inspirational trailblazers like Ivette Soler—author of *The Edible Front Yard: The Mow-Less, Grow-More Plan for a Beautiful, Bountiful Garden*—some brave souls are taking front-yard gardening a step further and using their sunny front yard to plant edibles. Interspersed with ornamentals, or on their own, there is no reason to banish plants to the backyard simply because you can eat them. As Ivette cautions in her book, structure and hardscape keep a front-yard food garden from looking messy and upsetting the neighbors.

Commandment 5: Thou shalt plant in groups of three or five, never one.

Sweeps and swaths, multiples of the same plant—these are the elements of a well-designed garden, or so we're told. Onesies are frowned upon, as they create chaos. We should plant in groups of three, or better yet five or even seven. Wait a minute! How can you hope to have room for all the cool plants if you do it that way?

I suppose this is a good guideline if you aren't planning on buying a wide variety of plants, or for those who have a large garden and a budget to go with it. However, if you're a beginning gardener who wants to plant a little bit of everything, a gardener who's short on cash and has to carefully budget for each plant purchase, or even a rare plant collector, gardening by the rule of threes and fives can feel rather discouraging.

As a result of my passionate plant acquisitions, I'd resigned myself to having a "collector's garden," a label that left me feeling a little less-than—like my garden was nice, but with an asterisk. Try

Top: Repeated elements in my front garden include a pair of *Yucca rostrata* plants, a few meandering specimens of *Juniperus conferta* 'Blue Pacific', and similarly shaped agaves and opuntias.

Bottom: Why plant just one *Agave ovatifolia* 'Frosty Blue' when you can go double for twice the effect? Good old Mother Nature planted the three *Euphorbia rigida*—perfectly spaced in front of my house—and I couldn't resist adding another *Yucca rostrata*.

to picture a collector's garden. Close your eyes and conjure up the image. It looks a little like a group photo with each person dressed in clashing colors and competing patterns, right? When every plant is a potential star, how do you create harmony? The light went on for me during a conversation with a friend. She was ruminating on the design of her garden and said something about the need to repeat plants, "as you do so well." What? I have a collector's garden, random and unorganized! Then she started naming off all the plants that are repeated across my garden: *Yucca rostrata, Euphorbia rigida, Dasylirion wheeleri, Hakonechloa macra.* Not in sweeps and swaths, but peppered throughout, creating a different kind of overall unity.

When you choose one or two plants—a grass, or a simple yet sculptural yucca—and dot them throughout the garden, your eye picks up on the pattern, and the garden feels unified. Then you can indulge your plant lust and fill in the remaining spaces with one-off obsessions. Another approach is to repeat colors, such as luscious dark-leaved plants; textures like big leaves; or forms like a tall pencil cypress or other columnar trees. As I've discovered, the important thing is to identify an element you like and repeat it.

Commandment 6: Thou shalt create pathways where two may pass.

Garden pathways should be easy to navigate, and for many that means building them wide. Room enough for two people to walk side by side is a frequently cited minimum, but why? This standard may be desirable in a public park, but in a private garden, especially a small one, that seems like wasted space. Perhaps the concept came from people who don't like to feel plants touch their skin as they pass by? I'll admit I'm more forgiving than many when

This pathway—in the English garden that inspired the blog *Alternative Eden*—wouldn't be nearly as enticing if it were four feet wide. A narrow pathway ensures the plants are part of the experience of getting there.

plants encroach on my personal space. However, if all my pathways were four feet wide, that would severely reduce my available planting space. Thinking about how family and friends move through the space, the only time wider pathways would be useful is when the garden is open for a tour—and that only occurs once or twice a year. Why build for the exception?

Commandment 7: Thou shalt group plants with similar needs.

It seems logical to put plants with similar cultural needs together, right? In fact, it's vital to the health of your plants that you meet their requirements. However, I like to mix and match a bit, explore the contrasts. If you include containers in your garden there's a way around this rule, especially when it comes to water use. In my garden, I've planted a dry-loving *Agave ovatifolia* 'Frosty Blue' next to a stock-tank pond filled with gallons of water. Water lilies bloom next to agave spikes, and bog-loving carnivorous sarracenias tower over them both. These plants all love the sun but they have different water and soil requirements. Since they're kept happy in separate containers, they get as much, or as little, water as they like and still manage to read like a cohesive planting.

There are ways to play with light requirements, too. Sun-loving plants can't be cheated out of their much-needed light and stay happy. They do cast shade however—and the larger the plant, the bigger its shadow. Tucking a shade-loving ground cover, or smaller perennial, under a shrub is a great way to maximize the planting space, while also expanding the range of plants you can grow in your garden. For this approach to be successful, make sure the plants' moisture requirements are similar.

Commandment 8: Thou shalt not kill a healthy plant.

You inherit a new-to-you garden and survey your empire: all you see is pink. The previous gardener loved pink flowers but you most definitely do not. What to do? Hide them with more plants? Cut off the buds before the flowers open? Deny them water and hope they'll just die quickly? Obviously, these are not great solutions (well, the last one might deserve a second look). But here's something I discovered: it's okay to get rid of perfectly healthy plants when they don't match your vision. Gardeners are nurturers, and as a plant lover, this may be hard for you to swallow. However, once

A mix and match of plants that prefer dry conditions and those that like it wet can coexist when they're grown in containers.

you do, you'll never look back, I promise. If the plant isn't making you happy, get rid of it!

You may be surprised to learn there are people willing to adopt your castoffs. Online communities and free listings are a great way to get rid of plants, just like old furniture. Even better, form a group that meets occasionally to swap plants—you divest yourself of plants you don't want and acquire new ones—all for free.

While re-homing a plant is ideal, it isn't always possible, especially if you overplant like I do. Plants grown on top of each other, with roots comingling, don't typically allow for digging out a root ball large enough to ensure successful transplanting. Even worse, you could damage the roots of a plant you wish to keep. Sometimes you just have to chop out the plant you don't want and throw it in the compost—and that's okay too. Really!

About Those Gardening Commandments

The stunning flowers and cinnamon-colored buds of *Magnolia laevifolia*, a plant I once loved but chose to yank after an ice storm bent the trunk into an awkward shape.

A word of caution before you get too carried away with that shovel. Unless you're in possession of an unlimited amount of time and money, you probably don't want to wipe out an inherited garden all at once. Creating a new garden can be expensive and time consuming. By tearing out and rebuilding your garden in stages, you can make thoughtful decisions and prioritize your expenditures. It took me nine years before I'd redone every section of my small garden, saving for last the removal of an ugly, overgrown hedge and the building of a fence. My inherited roses, azaleas, and daisies were yanked within weeks of moving in. Along with a pair of *Pieris japonica* plants, the last "builders' special" pink rhododendron from the 1950s didn't get removed until eight years into working on my garden. In my new garden (filling up with lots of exciting but small plants), I valued these handed-down shrubs for their mature size, even if I didn't particularly care for the plants themselves. Through careful pruning, they gained a semi-attractive shape, and I managed to overlook their negative qualities until the time was right to replace them.

Here's a sad truth: it's not always came-with-the-house plants that require tough choices. Sometimes it's a plant you once loved that needs the heave-ho. I walked into my back garden one spring day and my gaze fell upon a *Magnolia laevifolia*. I'd hunted for that plant, nurtured it, and watched it grow to a five-foot-tall shrub. But now it was awkward, and—thanks to a winter ice storm—slightly bent. Sizing it up that day, there was no denying that it detracted from the garden rather than adding to it. I'd been unconsciously averting judgment for quite some time, as though by ignoring the magnolia, it would magically fill out and take a more graceful shape. Examining the fat, cinnamon-colored buds about to burst into perfect white flowers, my heart hurt, but I knew it had to go. Do I regret making the choice? Not for a minute. I let the flowers bloom and enjoyed them to their fullest. Then the whole thing went into the yard waste bin, and I never looked back. It was the right decision to make and it allowed me to move forward with a new planting scheme for the space.

A NOTE ABOUT BOTANICAL NOMENCLATURE

People have very strong feelings when it comes to using common plant names versus botanical names. I've been teased for my insistence on using botanical names and—on more than one occasion—accused of being pretentious. So why do I do it? Because I love the certainty these names provide, even if I can't always pronounce them correctly. I know it's frustrating when you're plant shopping and have no idea what all those randomly jumbled letters on the label actually mean. Learning botanical nomenclature takes time. However, you may discover it's a handy tool that unlocks a treasure trove of information on each plant. Common names can be applied to more than one kind of plant, and are often regional. For example, the common name "hens and chicks" can refer to varieties of two different genera: *Sempervivum* and *Echeveria*. Sempervivums are alpine plants, many hardy to below zero degrees Fahrenheit (F). Echeverias are Central American succulents that can only tolerate a light frost, at best. Using the botanical name alleviates unnecessary confusion about the plant to which you are referring. Keep at it; you'll pick up botanical speak faster than you think possible.

CREATE A GARDEN YOU LOVE

I f your garden doesn't bring you joy, what's the point? It sounds so simple, but sometimes we forget that pleasing ourselves is reason enough to do something.

Pearl Fryar, the man upon whom the 2006 documentary *A Man Named Pearl* is based, summed up his gardening philosophy with these words: "Most people garden for other people. But I garden for Pearl. My garden looks like me—my thinking, my ideas, my life." When you garden for yourself, creating your own personal vision of paradise, you're free to plant petunias in old tires and surround your cactus with white gravel. Or if you're Pearl, you take your three acres and create a topiary sculpture garden that people drive hundreds of miles to see.

I look back on early photos of my garden and I cringe at some of the plant choices I made and the combinations I came up with. Then I remember how much I loved that bright pink caladium, and so what if the first agave I planted was backed by an *Acanthus mollis*, a strange and doomed combination if ever there was one. I was surrounding myself with plants that made me happy, and I was learning in the process. No one is born a Master Gardener. We all learn by doing, reading and watching, asking and listening—but mostly doing. In this chapter, I'll share a few design ideas and bits of wisdom I've acquired as I built the garden I love.

The Best Gardens Reflect the Taste of the Gardener

Even though it was never meant as a focal point, there's a small vignette in my front garden that draws a lot of attention, and not always positive. It came about as an accident when I re-homed an inherited peony (its hot-pink flowers needed to flash their voluptuous petals elsewhere). Apparently, I left a small chunk of the tuber behind in the original place. In less than a year, the plant was back and blooming. But before it made its presence known—thinking I'd gotten rid of the peony—I'd planted a freebie prickly pear cactus (*Opuntia*) nearly on top of it. The resulting mash-up—as both plants claimed the space—was so unexpected, yet so completely wonderful, that I left it, especially once I discovered they didn't seem to mind sharing the spot. While the combination of prickly pear and peony may not be everyone's idea of "visually pleasing," it works because they have similar needs: lots of sun and well-drained, or at least not water-logged, winter soil. This vignette also serves as a

Previous: Who says palm trees don't belong in Portland? This *Trachycarpus fortunei* looks right at home in my garden.

Peter Herpst has planted and curated a garden filled with elements he loves, including a *Corylus avellana* 'Contorta' draped with *Tillandsia usneiodes*, Spanish moss. The local exotic birds seem to like it, too.

sort of litmus test for designer types who visit my garden. Do they look at it as a warning that they're dealing with someone who has questionable taste? Or do they smile and appreciate the unexpected? I've seen both reactions flash across their faces. As for me, I've come to terms with the peony's hot-pink flowers.

It's not uncommon for people to move to Portland and promptly tear out mature palms like *Trachycarpus fortunei* because they are under the impression palm trees don't belong in Oregon. Of course, it's their garden to do with as they like. Still, the notion of a particular plant not belonging when it's obviously doing just fine is bizarre. It belongs if you want it there.

It isn't always plantings that stir questions of good garden taste. While I prefer to fill my garden with plants and colorful pots, there are many gardeners who feel a garden isn't complete until you've added art—be it original works by real artists (art with a capital "A"), or a collection of eclectic pieces assembled over the years. Like plant choices, I think art that reflects the personality of the owner is what feels the most authentic and successful, whatever form that may take.

CREATING A VERY PERSONAL GARDEN

My friend and fellow garden blogger Peter Herpst (outlawgarden.blogspot.com) is a natural-born collector and his garden reflects his many passions. The way he layers plants and unassumingly tucks in rare specimens is masterful. If you were handed a list of the plants in his garden, you'd probably estimate its size to be at least an acre, maybe two, but it measures just over a quarter acre—a large city lot in Tacoma, Washington.

Looking beyond the plants (which is no easy feat), what makes Peter's garden unique is how perfectly it reflects his personality. His is an eclectic garden with cast-off tombstones requisitioned as pavers, bowling balls repurposed as edging material, and a fire pit with flames of red glass and dark canna lily leaves. It simply could not have been created by any other gardener.

What might have been just a simple brick pathway in another garden is interspersed with decorative glasswork insets. A path of crushed glass snakes through tall arching bamboo and colorful glass balls float inside a huge cracked "dinosaur egg"—all clues that Peter is also a talented glass artist. There's even a throne (a wicker king chair) where he can sit and take it all in; not that he does much sitting in his garden.

Clockwise from left:

It's not every garden that has a nude, angel-winged mannequin to help with clean-up chores.

Decorative glasswork adds color to a simple brick pathway in Peter Herpst's garden in Tacoma, Washington.

Collected bowling balls surround a planting of *Ophiopogon planiscapus* 'Nigrescens'.

Inspired by similar spheres in the garden of famed artists and gardeners George Little and David Lewis, Peter discovered—through trial and error—how to create "dinosaur eggs" for his own garden. The blue one is his handiwork.

Successful Gardeners Kill Plants and So Will You

I've encouraged you to go ahead and kill a plant you don't love. But here's the thing: you're going to kill plenty of plants you do love. Sometimes you'll be able to identify why, other times it will be a mystery, and it won't always be your fault.

On the day before a big group was due to tour my garden, I discovered a large shrub, my *Grevillea victoriae* 'Murray Queen', had gone crispy—dead, quite literally overnight. *Grevillea* is a genus in the Proteaceae family, and as a friend said when I mentioned the tragedy on social media, "Proteaceae like to die. It is their very favorite thing to do." I knew he was right, because it had happened before with two other grevilleas, but back then I didn't have a tour coming through my garden the next day. What to do? Knowing the group consisted of real dirt-under-their-nails gardeners, I left the dead shrub in place and we talked about it. They were great people and totally understood; laughs were had by all, even me. After they left, I tore out the dead grevillea and stuck a large container of canna lilies in its place.

Plants that up and die after living a long and healthy life are one thing, but as the late J. C. Raulston, the horticulturist and founder of North Carolina State University's legendary arboretum said, "If you are not killing plants, you are not really stretching yourself as a gardener." Experimentation is at the core of building a garden. It's only through trial, error, and dead plants that you discover what works. I like that. How can we expect to get it right the first time, every time? Take cooking for example. It may take a little finessing to get a new recipe right, we all accept that. If the first time you tried baking chocolate chip cookies, they had all ended up flat and

Top: My *Grevillea victoriae* 'Murray Queen', bent under a heavy load of ice. Although it made a quick recovery, the ice incident may have been one of the factors that led to the plant's demise.

Bottom: There are so many different shapes and colors of agaves to choose from. *Agave bovicornuta*, with its orange spines, makes a spiky statement in the garden of Gerhard Bock.

burnt, would you have given up and never baked them again? What a shame that would be!

Your Garden Will Evolve

As gardeners, we seem to follow a certain path of development. I became aware of this pattern one spring when every single plant I was drawn to was a shrub. I was obsessed. For the longest time, I gardened only with perennials, and tender ones at that. Going back further, I went through a grass phase and a bulb phase—stretching way back, I even had a pretty-flower phase. I've never gone through a tree phase though, mainly because I think young trees look goofy, I'm too impatient to wait, and I've never had the budget for big trees. That's a blessing in disguise because I want all the sun I can get, and trees inevitably cast shade. Why the sun craving? Because of my ongoing agave phase of course!

Everyone's gardening journey is different, and the available space we have to garden changes over the years. After all, most of us don't start off in our twenties with a house on plantable land. It's natural that our plant palettes evolve. As we grow older, our disposable income goes through peaks and valleys; there are times we're able to spend more on plants than others. In addition, we travel and learn and are exposed to different types of plants.

I still remember the awe I felt when I learned there were so many different kinds of agaves, more than just the big blue *Agave americana* or the small artichoke agave, *Agave parryi*. There were green ones and gray ones, variegated ones, ones with no spines, and ones with orange spines. It was like a chocolate lover discovering there's more than just grocery store chocolate to be had. The possibilities! Loving and learning about plants is a never-ending adventure of discovery.

A friend once mentioned that gardeners go through an evolutionary process: from annuals to perennials, to shrubs and trees, and eventually to conifers. She speculated that we are simply in the grip of some Darwinian phases over which we have little control. A current obsession of mine reverses that size continuum. At the moment I'm intrigued by small ferns and mosses—the kinds of plants that tend to grow on other plants or can be found tucked in tiny spaces, even on hardscape. I'm still infatuated with shrubs, though, and the only factor that's slowed my acquisition is the fact I have little space left in my garden.

I'm also drawn to big leaves that make people stop and stare. There's something primordial about them, something jungly. *Tetrapanax papyrifer*, the rice paper plant, is a favorite. It has huge, deeply folded, palmate leaves up to three feet across, which sprout atop tall, sometimes branching, bare stems. They are simply gorgeous. After an unsuccessful first attempt (I planted too late in the fall for the plant to become established before winter), I am thrilled to finally have the tetrapanax clump of my dreams anchoring a corner of my front garden. It's one of my most asked about plants, and kids especially love looking up at the giant leaves.

Imagine my surprise, while chatting with a knowledgeable nurserywoman one day, when she declared that "tetrapanax is definitely not a front yard plant." I should note she'd never visited my garden, so she had no idea she was commenting directly on my plant choices. I had to pause before I could casually ask why. I expected to hear how the powdery indumentum found on the underside of the leaves is an allergen, or how the plant's tendency to send out runners makes it a badly behaved garden thug. That wasn't the case; her reasoning came down to aesthetics. A plant which called that much attention to itself just wasn't appropriate

for the front yard. It was too dramatic and needed to be put in the back garden where it could be "discovered" and didn't outshine the other plants. Too theatrical for the front garden—who knew? I'm still working through that one; not sure I'll ever be able to agree.

Another group of plants often labeled inappropriate for the front garden is within the genus *Euphorbia*. All euphorbias release a toxic latex sap when their stems—and sometimes their leaves—are broken. I'm reminded of an incident in which a gardener I know was lectured by a passerby about how dangerous "those plants" were, and how dare she plant them in her front garden—where children could come in contact with them. I would have been tempted to reply "how dare your child come in contact with my plants." Still, it's a point worth considering. I plant what I want but

Towering *Tetrapanax papyrifer* anchors a corner of my front garden. Too dramatic? Never!

keep euphorbias and sharp plants well back from walkways. You want visitors to enjoy your garden, not take an unexpected trip to the emergency room.

Another consideration when it comes to front yard plantings is vandalism. Plant theft, flower picking, and containers disappearing overnight—these things have happened to me, and you should be prepared for them to happen to you. One kind-hearted friend says, "I guess they needed those blooms more than I did." I'm not that forgiving, but I do keep on planting, and I find the people who stop to admire and ask questions make it all worthwhile. Truly one-of-a-kind plants, or containers light enough to easily walk away, are tucked out of sight and out of temptation's way.

Not Every Garden Needs to Be a Flower Garden

I'm a foliage gardener. It's the leaves that get me. I do grow a few plants for their blooms, but the majority earn a place in my garden because of their foliage. That must make my garden rather boring right? Green blob after green blob? Not at all, thanks to mixing and matching small leaves with big leaves, different shades of green, and different textures, like tough agave leaves combined with the feathery foliage of *Amsonia hubrichtii* (threadleaf bluestar).

You aren't skimping on color if you're gardening with foliage instead of flowers. Color is an important design element in the foliage garden. Plants come in a wide spectrum of greens—from chartreuse to dark, almost black, as well as silver, gray, purple/burgundy, and even pink. Variegation adds another layer of texture with stripes, dots, and mottled or uneven patterns in two or

Texture takes over when color is absent. Different shades of green and varied leaf shapes keep this part of my garden from fading to blah.

more colors. There is a trick that designers use to ensure a garden includes enough foliage types to be visually interesting: take a black and white photo. When all color is removed you can easily identify where plants fade together, where your eye may read them as a green blob and increased contrast is needed, and where varied foliage sizes and textures successfully create distinction and visual interest.

Even where foliage is king, flowers are unavoidable. While distinctive foliage may be the reason you acquired that certain treasure, plants do want to bloom. For example, the gorgeous powdery blue leaves of *Hosta* 'Samuel Blue' are lovely in their own right, so who needs an anemic flower ruining the picture? When I simply can't tolerate a plant's flowers, I cut them off. Done. Sometimes they end up indoors, in a vase, but not always. Don't be afraid to cut the flowers and garden just for the foliage.

I also think it's okay to leave a little turf. Popular opinion among the plant-crazed is that lawns are wasted space, ground which could be better used for mixed plantings. I've removed most, but not all, of my lawn—some of it remains. Why? While I encourage getting rid of the great American front lawn, a patch of turf gives your eyes a place to rest. It's a solid green negative space to counter the exuberant plantings. And yes, I said green. I irrigate my lawn in the summertime. It's small and since it's surrounded by perennials, shrubs, and trees, it's safe to assume that when I'm watering the lawn, I'm also watering these plants. In addition, that bit of green grass has a cooling effect on a hot day and it's a great place for sprawling out and relaxing in the sun, for both humans and pets.

When the time came to define my back garden borders with edging material, I longed to use thin Corten steel strips. They were very popular at the time. They looked so modern: crisp and clean—and they were metal. I do love metal. Several gardeners whose style I admired used Corten; theirs were custom fabricated, cut to length, with bonded corners. Long story short, I had no idea where to get such a thing made and I was pretty sure it wasn't in my budget anyway. That was a blessing in disguise.

Since I'm a firm believer in the consistency of materials and had already planned to build a patio and path of gray concrete pavers, I decided my edging material would be gray bricks. They were cheap, readily available, and I could install them myself over time. So what was the blessing? After installing the first section, I discovered the

YOUR CAMERA IS A GARDEN TOOL

While some say the garden journal is dead, I say it's just moved onto your computer. If I have any regrets, it's that my early gardening efforts were rarely recorded. Back then, my phone was only a phone, and I didn't always have a camera in my pocket. It's so easy to record my garden now. Take advantage of this and snap copious amounts of photos. Your camera is the best tool you have to really see your garden. We become blind to the familiar; when you see the same thing every day, it's hard to look at it with a critical eye. Taking a photo and looking at it on a screen, you'll notice things you otherwise would not have. Plus, it's a great way to track a plant's growth or take your garden with you to the nursery.

brick's flat, narrow edge was the perfect width for a lawnmower wheel. I could mow the lawn, right up to the planting area, and had a solid surface to guide me. Plus, mine is a garden lacking in space and the lawn has steadily been shrinking as the planting beds have been growing. It is a breeze to pull out the brick edging and reconfigure it whenever I want to expand a planting area. The metal strips, in contrast, would have been fairly permanent. I like the look of the brick too, especially as it's aged and acquired a patina.

Whether you settle on metal strips, rocks, flexible plastic pieces, a deep furrow in the soil, or no edging at all, I share this tale to encourage you to come up with an answer that works for your unique situation. You may stumble upon your own inspired solution with hidden benefits that reveal themselves over time.

Gray bricks laid end to end and buried level with the surrounding ground create a solid border between the lawn and my planting beds.

Cramscaping: Leave No Ground Bare

"If I look at my garden and see dirt, then I know I still have room to plant," says a gardening friend of mine. While there are people who don't like their plants to touch—ever—that's not a style of gardening I can recommend. Who wants to look at bare ground or mulch? Aren't layers of plants more interesting? There's a labor benefit too. By covering every bit of exposed soil with plants, you're keeping down the weeds. Less time weeding means more time enjoying your garden.

So, what is cramscaping? It's the fine art of cramming as many plants as possible into a landscape. I cramscape because my garden is small and I want to grow all the plants I possibly can. By employing a densely layered style with plants of varying heights (from ground covers, perennials, and shrubs, up to tall trees) all planted one on top of the other, I'm able to squeeze in more plants per square foot. It's a happy day when I look at a shrub and realize it's grown enough that the bottom few branches can be pruned, making room for a ground cover or small perennial to be planted under it. Two plants in the space of one: a cramscaper's dream come true!

If cramscaping sounds unnatural, just think of the cliché "nature abhors a vacuum" and how quickly opportunistic weeds take over a bare spot of land. Nature is the original cramscaper—gardening on the wild side. Of course, not all climates are conducive to this style of planting. In the desert for example—where water is scarce and plants compete for this vital resource—the cramscaping style is probably not suitable.

In the early years of a garden, when plants are small, cramscaping helps to create the illusion of a more mature landscape because plants cover all the ground. I intentionally overplant with the knowledge that eventually, as they grow, some plants may need to be removed. As I discovered by accident, cramscaping has another benefit—when a plant up and dies, you're not left with an obvious hole as the surrounding plants quickly fill the void.

The ultimate in cramscaping is using one plant to support another. For example, vines provide a second layer of interest and take up no garden space if they're allowed to grow through the structure of an existing plant. I once grew an evergreen *Clematis armandii* 'Snowdrift' through a giant mophead hydrangea. I hated how bare the hydrangea was for nearly half the year; the fast-growing clematis solved that and gave me fragrant flowers as a bonus. Of course, I created a labor nightmare when the time came to prune the hydrangea. I eventually realized the better

Left: *Passiflora lutea* and an unidentified species of *Bomarea* climb the trunk of my *Trachycarpus fortunei*.

Right: Peter Herpst adds a little summer color to the trunk of his *Trachycarpus fortunei* by tucking in various tillandsia and other epiphytic bromeliads.

solution was to just remove the hydrangea and replace it with an evergreen shrub, or two, and low-growing ferns—more plants is always the right answer.

Those accustomed to the iconic bare-trunked palm tree look of *Washingtonia robusta* may find that the hirsute trunk of *Trachycarpus fortunei* (hardy windmill palm) takes a little getting used to. The fuzz, however, is quite convenient for growing things up and tucking plants into. My tallest specimen of *T. fortunei* supports two different vines; both of them die back to the ground in the cooler months, so there's no concern of losing the palm under a tangle of foliage.

If I gardened in a warmer climate than zone 8, my palm's fuzzy trunk would be treescaped: covered with multiple tillandsias and other bromeliads. These epiphytic plants can be tucked into the palm trunk's fibers and small pockets at the base of the fronds. Eventually they secure themselves with their own clinging roots. Since winter cold makes this impossible in Portland, I drape these epiphytic growers around the garden in the summer months and bring them indoors for the winter.

A word of caution about overplanting. In any plant community—be it naturally occurring or manmade—there will be plants that grow faster than others. Some plants will thrive, some will disappear. I've had

WHAT IS AN EPIPHYTE?

"Did you hear about the argument between a tillandsia and a bromeliad over the best seat on the branch? No? One jumped on the other and it turned into an epifight— get it? Epiphyte!" Husband humor.

An epiphyte is a plant that grows on a surface, such as a branch, of another plant. The word comes from the Greek *epi*, meaning "upon" and *phyton*, meaning "plant." Epiphytic plants absorb nutrients and sustenance from the air, rainwater, and debris that collects on the host plant. The host plant is there only for support; the epiphyte is not parasitic and does no harm to the host.

hostas shaded out by aggressive ferns, and eryngiums that gave up the ghost when a grevillea won the battle for space. If I really wanted to save the less robust plant, I could dig it up and move it to a better location. Sometimes I do. Sometimes I just like to see how a patch of garden transforms over the years, without any interference from me, even if that means losing plants.

Plants growing on plants aren't limited to just vines. In warmer parts of the world, it's not uncommon to see an opuntia (prickly pear cactus) sprouting out of the crook of a tree, or on an ivy-covered fence. At the Ruth Bancroft Garden, there are several *Cereus hildmannianus* plants growing out of a *Butia capitata* (jelly palm). While it's tempting to think this smile-inducing treescaping was done by the garden's staff, that's not the case according to curator Brian Kemble. He credits the planting to birds that ate the cactus seed and then perched in the palm and distributed the seed. Brian adds, "This is obviously not a good long-term choice of a growing spot, since the cactus gets to be several tons in time."

After spotting a tiny epiphytic plant (possibly *Utricularia alpina*) growing in a bromeliad at the Amazon Spheres, I was inspired to try it myself with a small *Lemmaphyllum microphyllum* (bean fern). The plant is epiphytic, but since it came planted in soil, I didn't want to destroy the existing roots. I wrapped its small root ball in sphagnum moss and tucked it into a leaf base of one of my larger bromeliads. The possibilities are endless when you're playing with plants and cramscaping.

Top: Bird-planted *Cereus hildmannianus* (cactus) sprout in the trunk of a palm tree at the Ruth Bancroft Garden.

Bottom: *Lemmaphyllum microphyllum* grows in the leaf base of a bromeliad. Since it's an epiphytic fern, it doesn't harm the bromeliad.

COMBINING COLORS

Color guru Keeyla Meadows has created a garden that few people would describe as subtle, yet she combines bold, saturated colors in such a harmonious way that they never clash or try to out-compete each other. In her book *Fearless Color Gardens: The Creative Gardener's Guide to Jumping Off the Color Wheel*, Keeyla shares her secrets for working with color in a way that seems intuitive. She even advocates for control, writing, "Too many colors becomes very slippery, hard to handle, sliding right into a mud puddle of colors. Keep your palette simple, clear, and alert."

I've had the pleasure of visiting Keeyla's garden on a blazing hot day in June and a cool, sunny day in December. Her color choices remain vibrant and inspiring no matter the quality of light. The bold yellow and purple hardscape in a back corner of her garden works with and enhances the foliage and flowers without overpowering them.

Keeyla's front garden is a combination of lively containers, artwork, rocks large and small, and plants, all backed by a very colorful home. The neighborhood around her house seems to embrace the style. The fact that that she lives near Berkeley, California—"quirky Berkeley" it's been called—may help.

Clockwise from top left:

Narrow hellstrip plantings include colorful plants like *Yucca desmetiana* 'Blue Boy'.

Hardscape in bold yellow and purple coordinates with the plant pots and brightens up what could otherwise be a dark corner.

You can tell this is a well-loved sit-spot at the back of Keeyla's garden.

Even in the month of December, the front garden of Keeyla Meadows is quite colorful.

Controlling chaos with materials and color

I have an innate need for order. There are times when I wonder if this might be a character flaw. However, when it comes to gardening, I think of it as a handy way to control what could quickly become pandemonium because of my cramscaping ways and the resulting riot of foliage.

One of the ways I keep order in the garden is through the consistency of the materials I choose. The patio, retaining wall, pathway, and edging between the lawn and planting borders are all gray concrete. The same size and color of gravel is used as mulch in the front and back gardens, and most of my containers are topped with pea gravel mulch as well. All of the extra-large containers throughout the garden are galvanized metal stock tanks, and my vertical trellis material is nearly always rusty metal. I believe this consistency of materials keeps these items from claiming the spotlight, a role I want reserved for the plants. Any containers that make it into the garden are shades of black, brown, orange, chartreuse green, or turquoise, or are made of metal. I'm not fearful of color, but rather aware of its power.

Finding Your Own Style: Inspiration

I admit, it's a bit of a contradiction to say "plant what you love" and then expect your garden to have an overarching style—but I truly believe that's possible. Being a sponge for style inspiration helps. Back in the analog years—before the ease of storing digital images—I was an avid reader of magazines. Just reading a magazine was never enough, though. Images that spoke to me were torn out and pasted in empty journals or tucked into envelopes. I still have some of those pages. Very few of them are ideas I would consider implementing today, but identifying and studying images I found inspiring helped me to develop my own, albeit ever-evolving, style.

Sadly, the magazine industry has shrunk significantly—a sign of the digital times—but Pinterest and Instagram have made inspiring photos easier than ever to find and save. Books, garden blogs, and videos inform and inspire, typically with a distinct subject or point of view. Being a blogger myself I may be biased, but garden blogs are a great way to find your tribe of like-minded gardeners and connect with them across the globe. Knowledge and advice, which was previously passed on to beginners from gardening neighbors or acquired in the local garden club, is now easily found online.

On the other hand, when it comes to inspiration, there's nothing quite as exciting as visiting someone's garden in person. Walking through a space and immersing myself in the details, asking questions of the gardener, and taking photos I can refer to later, is my favorite way to be inspired (but please be sure to ask if it's okay before snapping those photos).

I'm part of a group that makes arrangements every year to visit private gardens. By walking through gardens I would never have found on my own, I've been exposed to many new plants and countless ideas. Gardens I've quickly dismissed as having nothing to offer have gone on to surprise me, and many times they've stuck with me in a way that a garden I thought I would love has not. By keeping your eyes and mind open, you never know what you might find.

How do you find open gardens to visit? Garden clubs and other social groups frequently open member gardens and organize fundraising tours; these are usually publicized through neighborhood organizations, newspapers, and other local media. Keep an eye out for yard sales and home-for-sale signs as well. I've visited all sorts of interesting gardens this way and sometimes even left with a gifted plant or two.

The Garden Conservancy also helps publicize open gardens in many states from spring through fall. You can search their website (gardenconservancy.org) by state, city, and month to find opportunities near you. This wonderful organization was founded in 1989 with the mission to "save and share outstanding American gardens for the education and inspiration of the public." The idea for the Garden Conservancy was born when Frank Cabot (the group's founder) paid a visit to Ruth Bancroft's garden and inquired about what would happen to the garden when Ruth was no longer around to care for it. Ruth did not have a satisfactory answer to that question. That's when the idea to start a nonprofit focused on garden preservation began. The Garden Conservancy has since grown into an association that helps formerly private gardens become community-based public resources and existing public gardens remain successful and sustainable.

Finally, visiting botanic gardens, in your hometown and when traveling, can spark creative thoughts. Botanic gardens employ professional staff and have large budgets to work with; the immersive experience these gardens provide can't be matched in a private garden. Wandering among the spiky, dry landscape at the Desert Botanical Garden in Phoenix, Arizona, transformed my perception of what a garden could be so fundamentally that my personal garden style was forever changed, even if it took me years to find the opportunity to integrate elements of what I'd seen there into my own garden.

A note on garden criticism

After touring a private garden with a small group, I was surprised to hear that some people found the garden jarring and unpleasant. When it came time for me to write my thoughts on the garden in a blog post, I wanted to mention this but then reconsidered. What if the garden's owner/creator read that some of our group didn't like her garden? I liked her garden, wasn't that enough? Praise flowed through my commentary and most of my readers' comments, but a few shared critical opinions. One commenter mentioned she hoped the gardener had been shielded from the negative comments. I hope that if the gardener read or overheard them, she let them roll right off her back. After all, part of gardening fearlessly is accepting that not everyone is going to like what you create.

EXPRESSING HER PERSONAL STYLE

When starting her second garden, which was much larger than her first, my friend Patricia Cunningham was unsure how to create a space that felt cohesive. Overwhelmed by all the open space and seemingly endless possibilities, she found herself engaging in a little plant retail therapy, and mentioned her dilemma to a local nurseryman. His simple suggestion was to "just pick a theme," to which Patricia replied, "I want to feel like I'm on vacation." Her vacation-themed garden was born.

Being a social person, Patricia designed a front patio where she could keep tabs on the neighborhood while enjoying her own garden—as well as the plants she'd snuck into her neighbors' gardens (with their permission, of course, at least usually). Tall, swaying grasses, numerous self-seeded *Eryngium agavifolium* plants, and fast-growing annuals like *Amaranthus caudatus* (love-lies-bleeding) provide some privacy screening.

Patricia's back garden was all lawn with tiny planting borders when she moved in. Now big-leaved tropicals like *Canna* 'Musifolia' (banana canna), *Musa basjoo*, and *Tetrapanax papyrifer* frame the space. Comfy patio chairs right outside the back door set the mood, along with several container plants. Island beds are filled with a mix of permanent plantings (*Lobelia tupa*, *Eucomis comosa* 'Oakhurst') and exotic annuals like bromeliads, while tall arching *Rhodocoma capensis* plants provide plenty of places for her dog Chiquita and playmates to hide.

While it may not come with a tropical temperature or beach, Patricia is happy with her stay-cay garden. "I've got a thing for plants that make me think I'm on vacation, and I like that I can then go inside and sleep in my own bed. Boring? Yes. But not entirely unsatisfactory . . ."

Clockwise from top left:

Musa basjoo and *Lobelia tupa* achieve jungle-like size in a single growing season.

Tall plants provide a feeling of privacy in Patricia Cunningham's otherwise exposed front garden.

All that's missing is a tall iced drink with a cocktail umbrella in it!

Big leaves and exotic flowers are the backdrop for a vacation-themed garden.

EXPLORE THE POSSIBILITIES

The British take gardening very seriously. Their Chelsea Flower Show is broadcast in prime time, and the Queen is certain to make an appearance. BBC programming includes several garden-themed television shows, and their presenters are celebrities. Therefore, when BBC television personality Monty Don said, "Half of gardening is just grown-ups going outside to play," I laughed out loud and then considered sending him a thank-you note. Gardening is exactly that. We get to be kids again, play in the dirt, pick the flowers, and climb the tree.

Previous: The bromeliad garden at Lotusland is both beautiful and fantastical.

The bold, colorful foliage of *Ensete ventricosum* 'Maurelii' added drama to my summer garden and provided support for the orange-blooming *Leonotis leonurus*.

The possibilities for fun and adventure in the garden are endless. Sure, there's raking and weeding, watering, mowing, and edging, but that's maintenance—repeated tasks, not unlike cleaning the house, only they're done outside and therefore are a little more enjoyable. Not unlike some homes, gardens can be treated like static creations. You can plant a tree and a few shrubs, put a couple of containers on the deck, and call it good. The plants will grow, maybe bloom, maybe die, but you don't have to change anything. You don't have to, but why wouldn't you? The fun part is when you get to rearrange the furniture (move some plants around), buy a new vase for the mantle (a new pot for the patio) and decorate for the holidays (put together a new vertical planting for the summer). If gardening was a "do it and be done with it" thing, I'd have gotten bored a long time ago. Instead, we get to constantly reinvent our gardens. In this chapter, I'll share some of my favorite ways to do just that.

Grow It as an Annual

As I've mentioned before, not every plant needs to be a lifetime commitment. It's okay to plant something knowing it will die with the arrival of winter—and I'm not referring to true annuals, plants that complete their life cycle in a single summer and die naturally at the end of the growing season. Instead, I'm referring to a plant that would live on for years in its ideal climate but will die off come winter in my zone 8 garden. In the nursery trade, these plants

My stock tank cutting garden produced the zinnias for this summertime arrangement. The *Melothria scabra* (cucamelon) vine, *Nicotiana* species, and foliage stems were also from the garden.

from a mail-order nursery—you know how persistent the spring catalogs can be.

Another tactic for squeezing in a few annuals is to grow them in a large container in a sunny location. In my case, that's a stock tank in my driveway. In lieu of a proper cutting garden, a couple of large containers of flowering plants can provide an entire summer's worth of vase material. The year I grew *Moluccella laevis* (bells of Ireland), I was enchanted for months by their twisting spires of green bracts.

Of course, if you're one of those lucky people with a large garden, this type of planning may not be necessary. If you're a small-garden cramscaper, however, it's all too easy to end up with no room for fun new annuals unless you plan for them.

By pollarding my *Cotinus coggygria* 'Royal Purple' each spring, I'm able to keep it sized right for my small front garden.

Coppicing and Pollarding

Some people regard coppicing and pollarding as plant abuse when these practices are actually longstanding methods used to, among other things, control the size of trees or large shrubs. Coppicing is the harsher treatment of the two; it involves cutting the tree back to ground level to stimulate new growth. Pollarding can best be described as hard pruning that keeps trees smaller than they would otherwise grow. Once a tree or shrub reaches its desired height, annual pollarding keeps it from getting larger. While both practices were historically based on the goal of producing new wood, that's not why I find them useful. My reasoning is twofold: first, by coppicing and pollarding, you're able to maintain plants at a smaller size; large trees that would otherwise overwhelm a small space stay sized "just right" so they can be cramscaped into urban gardens. Second, both practices produce foliage that is larger and sometimes more colorful than if the same plant were left to grow naturally. Dramatic foliage is a good thing!

One of the most common plants to receive this treatment is *Cotinus coggygria* (smoke tree). While many people cut it to the ground, I do drastic pruning in the pollarding style. By cutting the branches on my *C. coggygria* 'Royal Purple' back to a short trunk early in the spring, the shrub develops extra-large dark leaves on shorter branches. Unfortunately, hard pruning means sacrificing the plant's namesake "smoke"—the frothy effect that appears after the flowers on older growth fade—but that's a small price to pay for the bold foliage. My *Sambucus nigra* 'Eva' (Black Lace® elderberry) also responds to coppicing and pollarding with significantly larger foliage. As a bonus, its foliage stays at near eye level, where it's easier to appreciate.

I planted a *Paulownia tomentosa*, which has the potential to become the largest tree in my garden, because of its reputation as a fast grower—up to 10 feet in a season. I needed to block an unpleasant view and knew the empress tree would do the job quickly. I also have a slow-growing *Eriobotrya japonica* (evergreen loquat) which will eventually take over screening duty. Until then, the paulownia is pollarded at about 10 feet and grows to over 20 feet during the course of each season. Sometimes described as an exotic invasive, the empress tree does have a downside: its fragrant purple flowers go on to produce capsules containing countless tiny seeds, which disperse on the wind. Since the flowers form only on old wood, a pollarded tree never blooms and never produces seed.

The spectacular new growth and large leaves of *Paulownia tomentosa* provide a tall screen of foliage in a corner of my back garden.

Turning an Obstacle
into an Advantage

Sometimes our gardens present us with a design challenge that seems best solved by spending money, usually a lot of it. Thankfully, the expensive answer isn't the only one. An inspired solution often requires nothing more than creativity and maybe a little time.

Whenever I hear someone say, "Dead plants are opportunities!" I generally think they're referring to the joy of plant shopping, and the opportunity to buy more plants. However, faced with a dead tree in her new garden, a friend took that saying and turned it on its head. Instead of having the tree removed, she painted it blue and created a focal point—an opportunity to use what was there and honor the history of the garden, while saving the money that she would have paid to have the tree removed. Another person's approach was to collect colorful bottles, hang them from the branches, and slip their necks over small branch tips, creating a bottle tree.

Fern stumperies were popular in the Victorian era, and thanks to increased interest in ferns, they're in the midst of a revival. While a true stumpery may be a bit large for the average garden, there's no reason you can't devote a shady corner to a smaller version, especially when a single dead tree or several fallen branches can provide all the material you need to create one. Simply arrange the wood pieces in a way that creates hollows, which you'll use for planting. Different size branches, pieces of driftwood, or even decaying wood can be mixed in. If you're able to pull an entire dead stump free of the ground, its root structure not only adds intricate beauty but more planting pockets. A stumpery can be planted with ferns and other shade lovers, even bulbs—think of what you're

An underutilized corner at Portland Nursery became a fern planting with just a few logs and wood pieces to contain the soil and plants.

creating as imitating the forest floor. Small-space constraints should not deter creative solutions with fallen branches. The folks at Portland Nursery proved that by turning a corner of their shade-plant greenhouse into a small fern planting with logs and a little soil piled on a cement floor.

In my own garden, I dealt with the death of a multi-stemmed *Schefflera taiwaniana* by creating a "bromeliad tree" on the dead trunks. I wrapped the roots of small bromeliads with a little soil covered with moss or burlap and secured them to the trunks with wire. Wanting more space on which to work, I hauled home a couple of mossy branches I found on a walk, adding a horizontal structure on which more plants could be perched. A few tillandsias were an easy addition; they can be tucked in just about anywhere. Because I used plants that weren't winter hardy in my area, only a single summer's enjoyment was to be had from the creation, but it gave me time to evaluate what to plant in place of the schefflera. I avoided making a quick, potentially wrong, decision.

Turning an Obstacle into an Advantage

Opposite: A temporary installation of bromeliads on the branches of a mature shrub that died. Looking back on it now I can see so many things I would change, but I had fun making it, and that's what matters.

Right: Embracing the realities of her home in earthquake country, Jana Olson secured a "falling" container to the top of a cracked retaining wall and planted the whole thing with grasses and succulents. The final touch includes sections of ceramic bamboo and seedpod artwork from her friend, Berkeley artist Marcia Donahue.

More important, I had fun in the process and discovered that the location was a natural for bromeliads, so expanded their presence the following summer.

It's not always plants that fail. Faced with a cracked and leaning retaining wall, a Berkeley-area gardener decided to play with the fact that she lives in earthquake country, embellishing the wall rather than hiding it. To demolish and haul the concrete and debris away, not to mention building a replacement, would have cost hundreds, if not thousands, of dollars.

Turning an Obstacle into an Advantage

Vertical Gardening

A lot has been written on the subject of vertical gardening, and while its popularity may have peaked, I think there's still a lot left to explore. At its most basic, vertical gardening refers to a plant grown off the ground. Maybe its roots are in the ground, but the plant grows on a support system: a trellis, a fence, or another plant. Or maybe the plant, roots and all, are in a container suspended above the ground. Because they take up little to no ground space, vertical gardens can dramatically increase the real estate you have available for gardening.

Most people think of green walls when you mention vertical gardening. Those plant-covered surfaces are wonderful when they're done correctly, however, an entire green wall is beyond the DIY skills and budget of the average gardener. Done wrong, a green wall can be a costly mistake that damages surfaces and doesn't support the growth of healthy plants. Fortunately, there are easy alternatives that can be customized to your garden's features. Containers elevated above a planting bed add a layer of growing space and serve to highlight what's within them. Good old-fashioned hanging baskets or decorative hanging containers are vertical gardens at their simplest. These can be mounted off the side of a building, hung from a tree, or with a shepherd-style hook for freestanding support. I'll admit, traditional hanging baskets leave me cold; I prefer a modern glazed or metal container. For years, it seemed finding an attractive hanging container was nearly impossible. Thankfully, designers and makers have recognized the need and now there's no shortage of suitable options.

When there's nothing available from which to hang a planter, why not try the reverse and elevate it off the ground from below? My dish planter design—which I came up with after lusting for more

Clockwise from top left:

My hanging container collection includes the Point Pot from artist Dustin Gimbel and a charcoal-colored container from Target. My husband designed the agave gate and had it fabricated in Portland.

A green wall on Musée du quai Branly, in Paris, was professionally designed and planted by French botanist Patrick Blanc.

A trio of dish planters offers up an assortment of succulents for closer inspection. When winter weather arrives, I swap out these dishes for ones filled with hardier plants.

Clockwise from top:

Mounted bromeliads and expanded metal remnants hang on the fence behind our shade pavilion. Decorative containers, like the bright Circle Pot from Potted, are suspended beneath the pavilion roof.

My original bulletin board planter.

A closer look at one of the expanded metal panels hung on our fence.

expensive versions—does just that. The basic idea is a planting dish on a pedestal. In my case, the dish is the cover of a hanging chicken feeder, and the pedestal is a galvanized fence post cut to a specific length, but many similar things can be used. You could substitute a hubcap, a mixing bowl, or a light shade for the planter—or if you're really lucky, maybe you'll find an old rusty plow disc. The supporting base could be a length of metal pipe from a scrapyard, a piece of ducting, or even wood. What you plant in the dish will depend on the amount of soil it can hold, the drainage, and how often you're able to water. I started with succulents because my dish container didn't hold much soil and had a huge drainage hole. Eventually, I ventured on to small ferns like *Adiantum venustum* and even *Calluna vulgaris* 'Stockholm', a compact heather.

A sturdy fence can pull double duty if you mount or hang containers on it directly. Make sure the fence is strong enough to support the weight of a container and wet soil and, if you share the fence with a neighbor, be sure containers on your side won't negatively affect the durability of the fence or show unattractively on the neighbor's side.

I started hanging containers on a metal trellis when a vine I planted at its base refused to grow. Once I planted a second vine, which did finally take off, I didn't remove the containers—after all, cramscaping can go vertical too!

I dubbed one of the first verfical plantings in my garden the bulletin board, for the ease with which I could mount containers and change out the plants on it. The base is a panel of expanded metal sourced from a salvage yard. Currently, I've got two planters wired to its surface and tillandsias hanging on it. Because the bolts used to mount the metal don't move with the changing of the plants, they were completely sealed with silicone to prevent water damage to the wood siding.

A little hunting eventually led to an additional trio of expanded metal panels at a metal fabricator's scrapyard. I initially bought them to be used as simple trellises, but instead, they too have been put to work in the bulletin board manner. Their perforations allow for an always-changing variety of containers and plants to be displayed.

It may look decorative, but this section of wire fencing hung in our basement provides a winter perch for an assortment of tillandsias and other bromeliads. There's no reason why something useful can't be pretty, too.

Explore the Possibilities

Another vertical gardening project came about as a solution to a raccoon problem. The masked critters were taking nightly dips in my stock-tank pond. While the idea of them splashing about may seem quite entertaining, they were destroying potted plants as they dug in the wet soil, searching for tasty grubs. I determined their method of access was to jump into the water off a short retaining wall about a foot away. I needed a way to block them, and a roll of inexpensive wire fencing from the hardware store was the answer. It was easy to work with and placed against the edge of the stock tank it visually disappeared into the background—that is, until I decided to hang plants from it and made it a focal point. Another section of the same fencing was hung from the rafters in our unfinished basement. It became an indoor green wall on which I mount my collection of tillandsias and other hanging bromeliads when I bring them indoors for the winter. Giving the plants a good soak every other week isn't hard, because they are easily removed and rehung.

Crevice Gardening

I was first introduced to the tradition of crevice gardening when I visited a local garden designed by plantsman Sean Hogan, owner of Cistus Nursery in Portland, Oregon. A bend in a gravel path brought me face to face with a section of rock slabs turned on their side and buried in the ground. Agaves had been planted in between some of the slabs. How odd; I'd never seen anything like it and wasn't sure if I liked it. There were agaves, so that was a plus, but the rocks—what was up with them? I've since learned that this was an inventive way to make use of slate pieces from a demolished patio—and now, of course, I find myself intrigued by the possibilities.

My first crevice garden sighting, in a garden designed by Sean Hogan.

Since that first encounter, I've done additional research and learned more about crevice gardening than I dreamed possible. The concept is perfectly illustrated by the weeds that grow in the cracks of a sidewalk. Despite their apparently dire location, those weeds grow better than many plants in a garden. True crevice gardening involves placing rocks tightly together on end, with fissures between them. The fissures are filled with soil, and eventually with plants whose roots grow downward. The plants' roots stay cool and soak up water that funnels deep between the rocks, just like the cracks in the sidewalk. I said true crevice gardening because the experts are very strict about things like how close together the rocks should be and even what type of plants should fill the cracks. This type of planting can be traced back to the Czech Republic and an attempt to replicate the conditions that alpine plants need to thrive. Here in the United States, the area around Denver, Colorado, is the epicenter of crevice gardening.

Rock garden or crevice garden? Both! This unique garden is at Rare Plant Research in Oregon City, Oregon.

While the artistry behind a traditionally built crevice garden cannot be denied, there's no reason we can't take some of the ideas and translate them for use in our gardens. In my original example, vertically arranged rocks help increase drainage, a benefit when planting agaves and other dry-loving plants in a winter-wet climate. If you build with a significant amount of rocks and create peaks and valleys, these can actually increase the planting surface area of the garden. The varied topography also creates distinct microclimates, such as shady spots, where none previously existed. Crevice gardens don't have to be made from flat rocks, either. At Rare Plant Research, a wholesale nursery and private residence in Oregon, large boulders form an outsized crevice garden. Owner Burl Mostul sneaks in summertime bromeliad plantings from his nursery next to other plants that grow there year round.

ENCHANTED BY CREVICE GARDENS

Seen from the street, Carol and Randy Shinn's garden in Fort Collins, Colorado, is a beautiful mix of flowering perennials, shrubs, and a selection of conifers. There is a dry streambed and a meandering stone and gravel pathway. Once you walk up into the garden, however, you discover a series of crevice and rock gardens tucked in behind all those pretty flowers.

After moving to Colorado, Carol says she and her husband were naturally drawn to the rock yards in the area and began incorporating rocks into their landscape. Later, friends introduced them to the Rocky Mountain Chapter of the North American Rock Garden Society and they were hooked. In Carol's words, "Our ideas on rock placement gradually became more elaborate and sophisticated as we learned more." They built a horizontal crevice garden in the backyard, with the goal of mimicking layers of sandstone found in some areas of the West. Unfortunately, water drains off the ledges, instead of seeping into the cracks, which affects what can successfully be grown. *Arenaria* 'Wallowa Mountain' as well as various *Sempervivum*, *Jovibarba*, and *Sedum* species fill the horizontal cracks and manage to look lush, while also being drought tolerant.

Kenton J. Seth, a crevice garden construction expert, built two vertical crevice gardens for the Shinns' front garden. Carol especially appreciates the way multiple basalt pieces were laid to appear "nearly as one rock that had shattered." Kenton completed these gardens in the spring of 2014, so there's been ample time for the plants to fill in and look naturally at home, blending with the rest of the garden. According to Carol, a few of the many benefits of crevice gardens are that water soaks in but also drains well, so plants are less likely to be overwatered, and there's no frost heave in the winter. While there are fewer weeds, those that get a foothold are much more difficult to remove, she cautions.

Clockwise from top:

Walk into the Shinns' front yard and you'll discover this neat crevice garden, one of several on their property.

A closer look at just how narrow some of the crevices are in the Shinns' garden. The saxifrage is likely *Saxifraga paniculata* subsp. *cartilaginea* 'Foster's Red'.

A horizontal crevice garden in the Shinns' backyard.

For those who want to experiment with a crevice garden, but lack the space or desire to put together a full-size display, a small crevice garden in a trough-style planter is a creative solution. Or, if you have room for something a little larger, how about a crevice garden built with recycled concrete in stock tanks? While he relishes every opportunity to play with rocks, Kenton believes that recycled concrete will continue to grow in popularity and "level the playing field," as not everyone is able to easily acquire the quantity of rocks required to build a rock or crevice garden.

For a crevice garden in Grand Junction, Colorado, Kenton used just those materials: recycled concrete and stock tanks. Before filling the tanks with soil and concrete chunks, Kenton lined the walls with tar to keep them from rusting further—galvanized metal resists corrosion but can rust over time—and cut large holes in the bottom for additional drainage. If you're concerned you might have to do the same, let me put your mind at ease: I've had tanks in

Kenton Seth designed these crevice gardens in Grand Junction, Colorado. Using separate stock tanks allows for different soil mixes and thus more diverse plantings.

my garden for over 14 years and have never had an issue with them rusting through. A removable plug at the side of the tank, toward the bottom, ensures drainage, but you can create extra holes if desired.

Vignettes: Gardens within Gardens Pack a Punch

When you reflect on a garden that has inspired you, do you see the big picture, a sweeping vista, a panoramic shot? Or do you remember a detail, a plant combination, or a small section of the garden that stood out? Although I recall the overall impact a garden had on me, it's the vignettes I tend to remember the most. Details matter, and the little things add up. Vignettes encourage the viewer to stop and take note, which translates to memorability.

Because I've never gardened on an estate-sized plot, I have only the perspective of a small urban gardener. However, the areas of my garden that people seem to respond to most passionately are the small vignettes. Many of the design elements outlined in this chapter—a stumpery planting, vertical gardens, crevice gardens—naturally act as vignettes. By distributing these elements throughout your garden, you create focus gardens within the larger garden. As a result, the space feels much larger than it is. Vignettes, especially in hidden or screened parts of a garden, can answer a design challenge of how to include a type of planting that just doesn't seem to fit within the larger planting scheme. As your garden matures you may miss the process of designing and planting a new area; a vignette gives you an opportunity to play.

The dictionary definition of a vignette is "a picture (such as an engraving or photograph) that shades off gradually into the surrounding paper." When composing a garden vignette, imagine you're focusing your camera on a garden portrait: a picture within a larger scene; that's your vignette.

Putting together vignettes within the garden is a chance to be creative on a small scale. It's an afternoon or weekend project rather than an entire season's work. As summer wears on, I miss the rush of spring plant sales and new purchases, along with the sense of urgency to get them in the ground. Eventually the desire to create and plant hits me hard. The process—and it is a process—may start with a newly acquired plant (I enjoy going to nurseries year round). Or maybe it's a spur-of-the-moment stop at the salvage shop, where an interesting piece of metal starts my creative wheels turning. When these things come home with me, some go into the garden right away because I know instantly what I'm going to do with them. Others spend a little time in storage while ideas simmer.

There's a focal point vignette in the corner of my garden that has evolved into its current iteration over time. A trio of large galvanized containers has spent several summers in this spot, but what's in them changes regularly. Currently, they're filled with an *Agave americana* 'Variegata', an *Abutilon megapotamicum* 'Paisley', and a small *Mangave* 'Tooth Fairy'. The rusty metal additions started with a short planter—picked up at a reused materials art show and filled a year later with *Obregonia denegrii*, the artichoke cactus. Knowing the vignette needed more rust, I hunted down a rectangular metal piece and filled it with tiny agaves. A tall rusty cylinder came next. It stood empty for a while, until inspiration hit and I stuck an old metal funnel in the top, planted with a salmon-blooming *Aporophyllum* hybrid. I'm quite happy with this arrangement—but then again, a new discovery may have me changing things up next month. Vignettes don't have to be static creations or come together overnight—although sometimes they do.

One version of an ever-evolving vignette in my back garden. The plants in containers include *Agave americana* 'Variegata', *Abutilon megapotamicum* 'Paisley', and *Mangave* 'Tooth Fairy'.

THE DANGER GARDENETTE

Peter Herpst refers to his collection of potted succulents as his danger gardenette, a nod to my blog, *danger garden*, and my tendency to collect spiky plants in containers. By grouping these plants together in one sunny spot, he creates a vignette that is much more powerful than if he had dotted the containers throughout the garden. He says the collection first started out as "just three or four little plants on top of a table" but has grown to fill its designated space and then some.

In order to give the plants at the back of the arrangement a bit of extra height, Peter uses stacks of concrete blocks, hollow cylinders, and plant stands found on sale. He says, "It reminds me a bit of how a choir looks standing on risers or a staged family photo." He adds, "A few years ago, the Oregon Association of Nurseries used the line 'Don't just stand there, plant something!' in a lot of their printed materials. That's pretty much been my motto and would be my advice to anyone who wants to put together a vignette like this."

Clockwise from top left:

Your first glimpse of Peter Herpst's danger gardenette is slightly obscured by foliage.

Skeleton head beads are a spooky addition to sharp agave spikes.

The danger gardenette is arranged so that the plants toward the back are raised above those in front, on plant stands and stacks of other materials.

Much larger than the average home garden, Chanticleer is a 48-acre public garden in Wayne, Pennsylvania. Not a traditional botanic garden, Chanticleer is often described as a pleasure garden. A number of full-time gardeners work year round designing and maintaining their assigned section of the garden. While these areas are a bit too large to be considered a vignette, the fact that each is treated as its own garden within the larger garden highlights the similarities. The gardeners at Chanticleer are challenged to constantly change and improve their areas, and friendly competition is not unheard of. Doing a little research on the garden, I read a series of online reviews written by longtime lovers of the garden as well as people who had just discovered it. One person said it was "like being in a painting" and another noted that the grounds "included wonderful little surprises." Several reviews included the phrase "always something new to discover" and many people commented that the gardeners were extremely friendly and knowledgeable and seemed to genuinely enjoy talking with visitors. I can't help but think these gardeners are having a wonderful time because they're not just maintaining a garden, they're in a constant state of creating it. In the 2015 book *The Art of Gardening: Design Inspiration and Innovative Planting Techniques from Chanticleer*, horticulturist Dan Benarcik describes what they do as "gardening without a net." The book's author, R. William Thomas, goes on to say, "You might want to do the same in your own garden. Try. And try again. Continue what you like. Move to something else if you are displeased. Plant enough so the loss of one plant is not tragic."

I also find this quote from Monty Don to be rather inspiring: "It's quite common to see works of art in a garden and it's not very common to see gardens as a work of art." Seeing gardens as a work of art, how about that! Art is typically something visual—a painting, drawing, or sculpture—created by the human imagination, using talent and skill. Art is valued for its beauty and the thought-provoking emotional response it elicits. Why wouldn't a garden qualify?

Bringing the Garden Indoors

If you live in a climate with a winter season, you no doubt have a list of autumn garden chores. I call one of the more labor-intensive tasks on my list the Great Migration—the process of moving non-hardy plants in containers into the basement or under cover for the season. It's a lot of work, but it does mean many of my plants are indoors, where I am. As temperatures fall and we're spending less time outdoors enjoying what we've created, there are other ways we can appreciate our gardens in the off season.

I look at garden clippings as potential vase material throughout the year, but when a hard frost is in the forecast anything that might be frozen is fair game. Flowers I would never dream of cutting in September—for example, *Leonotis leonurus* (orange lion's tail)—are snipped without a second thought in late October or November. *Cyperus papyrus* stems and *Canna indica* leaves might fill a tall vase or two. I also like to experiment with blooms such as abutilon and passiflora.

If non-hardy plants have made it into the ground—ones I don't want to bother to lift and pot for overwintering—I might take cuttings and put them in a vase. If they root, I usually go ahead and pot them up. If they don't? Oh well, they were going to die anyway.

One autumn I waited too long to lift a group of succulents I planned to pot up. As I reached under the plants to tease them out of the soil, the tops just fell off in my hands—the stems had rotted from excessive rainfall. Rather than toss them, I nestled the tops in a shallow boat-shaped piece of pottery. The arrangement looked

great for weeks and became an unexpected Thanksgiving holiday centerpiece—guilt-free plant decapitation!

Hanging wreaths and leafy garlands, piling gourds and pumpkins on a table—there's no end to what gardeners can create from autumn's garden bounty. The winter holiday season is also a natural for garden decorating. More wreaths, decorated trees, vases filled with garden cuttings and evergreen swags.

Early spring means bringing forced bulbs inside, where we can experience their hopefulness up close. All these projects help gardeners in four-season climates remain connected to the garden throughout the year.

EXPAND YOUR OPTIONS WITH CONTAINERS

As a gardener who spent many years living in urban apartment buildings—apartments without balconies or other outdoor spaces of my own—I was frustrated. I yearned for actual ground in which to plant. As a result, I devised creative ways to indulge my passion without actual terra firma. My dad and I constructed custom window boxes for one apartment. I covered the back steps of another building with so many containers that fire safety became a concern for the upper floors. Still, as much as I loved my container gardens, I always longed to be a traditional gardener with soil beneath my feet.

Because container gardening was the only form of gardening available to me for so long, I always assumed I'd abandon the practice once I became a real gardener. Wait. Stop right there. Did I just write those words? Yes, I did. And that's how I really felt. I thought because I was planting only in pots, my type of gardening was somehow less authentic, that I wasn't a real gardener. I'm older and wiser now and have come to realize that container gardening is its own elevated form of gardening. It comes with many of the same challenges and rewards as an in-ground garden does, along with additional opportunities for exploration, experimentation, and creativity.

While I don't want to go back to gardening in containers exclusively, I'll never give them up. What was once a collection of a dozen pots has transformed into hundreds. The current container assortment ranges in size from a small pot that would fit in the palm of your hand, to a six-foot-long galvanized steel stock tank that would take a piece of machinery to lift. Without containers, my garden would be much less interesting and I would again be a frustrated gardener.

Previous: Planting in pots adds flexibility, allowing gardeners to tailor soil, growing conditions, and locations to best suit each plant.

Right: A small sampling of my ever-changing container collection.

Container Basics

Before we delve into the creative aspects of gardening in containers, let's cover some of the basics. It doesn't get much more basic than soil. To our plants, soil is everything. At the most elementary level, soil is the structure that surrounds the roots, which in turn provides support for the plant parts you see. The soil provides the nutrients the plant needs to grow (along with any added fertilizer) and it can retain a little, or a lot, of moisture. Unlike gardening in the ground, container gardening gives the gardener the chance to

control all the growing conditions. If you start out with a good soil mix tailored to the plant's needs, your container planting is set up for success. Some people mix their own potting soil; I buy it premade and add grit if better drainage is desired.

Even though it came without a drainage hole, I couldn't resist matching this handmade container with a cactus, *Stenocactus phyllacanthus*. A masonry drill bit took care of the no-hole problem.

One of the Gardening Commandments you may have heard relates to potting soil: we're told to never reuse it. When you empty a pot, you'd best get rid of the soil. But what exactly are you supposed to do with that soil? Small gardens don't have room for a mountain of old potting mix, and municipal yard waste programs typically ban soil from the materials they will accept. So I admit that I reuse my soil. I mix it with fresh, but unless the plant formerly living in the container had a disease or was infected by a garden pest, I see no reason not to reuse it.

Figuring out how to dispose of used potting soil is one concern. Another is money: let's face it, that stuff is expensive! Saving on the cost of purchasing additional potting soil is, in part, why people continue to fill large containers partway with nonorganic material such as packing peanuts. This practice also reduces the weight of a large container in case you may have to move someday. Without exception, every time I've done this I've regretted it. The plant sinks as the material settles, and the pot becomes top-heavy when the soil soaks up water and the other material doesn't. The only time I've had positive results using this method is when I was putting together a temporary planting in which the plant wouldn't be in the container longer than a single season and wouldn't be moved. My advice is to never buy a pot so oversized that you're tempted to fill it with anything but soil.

Which brings up the question of container size. Clearly, you don't want to transplant a newly purchased plant into a container smaller than the nursery pot it's growing in. Well, except when you do. Yes, this is another one of those Gardening Commandments that I break. When transplanting a new plant into a decorative container, generally you want to move up at least a few inches in size, adding room for the roots to grow. Sometimes, though, I really want a

UNUSUAL TOOL TIPS

I've put together an odd group of tools I find quite useful when planting or maintaining containers:

- Wooden skewers are inexpensive and work wonderfully for flicking debris out of cracks and crevices of succulents. I also use them to brace plants and plant parts while planting. They make great mini-stakes, too.

- A kitchen spoon allows you to get soil or gravel into tight spaces.

- Old paintbrushes do a fine job of cleaning soil off plants, especially succulents.

- A molded plastic dish drainer mat makes a great surface on which to work. The edge designed to let water flow into the sink works the same with soil when it's clean-up time. The other three, taller edges, contain the mess.

- Serrated steak knives work great for amputating agave leaves gone bad.

- No matter your age or fitness level, moving heavy containers can be a sure way to injure your back. Years ago, I purchased a device called the PotLifter; it distributes the weight to two people, not just one, and has handles that make it easier to grip a smooth-sided container. Do an online search and you'll find several different options for purchasing, or designing, your own.

Container Basics

plant to go in a specific container and if this means stripping away a little of the soil—and a few roots—to make it work, well, then, so be it. This is something you can safely get away with when planting succulents, because they store water in their fleshy leaves and aren't so dependent on their root system for hydration. I wouldn't treat a flowering perennial so roughly; they need all their accompanying roots.

As for matching plant to container, I employ the same concept I use when planting in the ground: I overplant or cramscape. Why use a container that won't be right-sized until a few years in the future? I prefer a more balanced look; you can always repot the plant into a larger container as it grows. In the case of some succulents, I pop them out of their containers periodically to root-prune them and add fresh soil. They get busy growing new roots and are

While this trio of *Agave utahensis* var. *eborispina* may appear too large to be crammed together in a nine-inch container, I transplanted them from small two-inch (plug-sized) pots—so it's a step up in size.

as happy as if they'd moved to a new—larger—container. Except they didn't, and I don't have to move around a bigger container.

Drainage is another important aspect of container gardening. Most decorative pots you'll buy come with a drainage hole. If they don't, you'll want to make one, and don't go small! Small holes are easily clogged. If the pot is ceramic or clay, I use a masonry drill bit to create one or more holes. I've used this method on several expensive pots over the years and never had one crack. If the container is metal, I use a hammer and a large nail to do the deed.

Once you've done what's necessary for excess water to escape the container, you'll want to make sure it drains away from the pot and doesn't cause staining on the surface underneath. Pot feet work great for this; they raise the container off the ground and allow for increased air circulation. You can buy fancy pot feet at any nursery, or make your own with small pieces of wood or plastic.

The Human Impulse to Garden

We humans have an undeniable instinct to surround ourselves with plants and to garden. Wherever we are—even in an office environment under artificial light—there will be plants. When circumstances don't allow for an in-ground garden, containers make it possible to garden on balconies and in tight spaces. Studies have shown that people who live in cooperative, assisted-living, and senior housing situations benefit from having the opportunity to garden. Renters, even those who rent houses with garden space, may prefer to keep all their plantings mobile and therefore use containers exclusively. As the traditional family home, surrounded by land and opportunities to garden, may not be the default housing solution for much longer, the future of container gardening seems bright.

THE FRUSTRATED GARDENER

T he *Frustrated Gardener* is the name of a garden blog written by Dan Cooper (frustratedgardener.com). Dan gardens in Broadstairs, a coastal town in eastern Kent, England, about 80 miles east of London. Why is he frustrated? Because he has "poster-sized ambitions" and a "postage stamp–sized" lot in which to realize them. Dan has two small gardens, distinct spaces separated by his home. Both gardens are lush flower and foliage paradises that disguise their small size and limited growing capability. The Watch House Garden, or Jungle Garden, measures 20 by 30 feet with two large raised beds along the outer walls. The rest of the garden is situated on a hard surface above an underground cellar. The newer Gin & Tonic Garden—acquired when Dan bought an adjacent cottage—is a 20-foot-square paved courtyard. Dan's answer to gardening under these conditions? Containers: 200 and counting.

Both gardens utilize a cramscaping philosophy and are living proof that you can create a stunning jungle garden out of nothing but containerized plants. Dan says there are definite benefits to this type of gardening, including the fact that "endless adjustments" can be made to be sure each plant is showing its best side and mixing well with its neighbors. "Once in situ, they can mingle, sprawl, tangle, and twist as much as they like, until the containers disappear from view and a junglelike effect is achieved." Rearranging of these pots continues throughout the summer. Dan has always favored containers in groupings, both for the way they look and because he feels plants are happier that way. "Grouped together they create a mini microclimate, they support one another, they shade each other's roots from the sun."

Clockwise from top:

The Watch House Garden is delightfully overgrown in September; the pathway from the outdoor kitchen to the dining table has almost disappeared.

Terra-cotta pots are Dan Cooper's preference for plant containers, thanks to their appearance, breathability, and weight.

Dan Cooper's Gin & Tonic Garden is lush in August.

Dan estimates about 90 percent of his containers are plain, inexpensive terra-cotta, as he prefers them for their "appearance, breathability, and weight." He uses large black plastic tubs for plants like canna lilies and gingers, because these can break through the terra-cotta with their strong roots. He avoids planting in containers with rims that curve inward: "It's devilishly difficult to get plants out of them."

Container gardening at this level is definitely not low maintenance, the plants have to be watered and fed regularly. Dan explains, "During the summer months, everything revolves around the needs of the garden: housework and friends are neglected, meals amount to toast, and watering is done in the dark. What the garden needs, the garden gets." Of course, the work is done willingly—for the most part.

The climate of Broadstairs compares to zone 9a in the United States, with Dan's own microclimate being closer to 9b. Frosts are rare; however, his gardens face east and when the wind blows from the east it is bitingly cold and dry, and pretty devastating. Dan lost a large *Lyonothamnus floribundus* subsp. *aspleniifolius* (Santa Cruz ironwood) when the wicked wind ripped it from one of the large raised beds.

With the purchase of the Gin & Tonic Garden, Dan inherited a greenhouse where tender plants can spend the winter. However, with limited space, if a plant is hardy its container stays in place over the winter months.

While gardening in containers may not be as straightforward as gardening in the ground, in no way should it be considered inferior. Besides allowing a plant to grow where it otherwise could not, Dan points out, "It allows plants to be treated as individuals, shown off when they are at their best, and hidden away when they tire." This kind of gardening offers the adventurous gardener endless opportunities to experiment. Dan adds, "Having gardened this way for so long, I no longer crave deep soil and huge borders. With a little thought, I can grow everything my heart desires in a pot, trough, or planter."

Container plants growing in the Watch House Garden include an assortment of big-leaf tropicals, gingers such as *Hedychium densiflorum* 'Stephen', and colorful coleus.

Containers Inspire Fearlessness

There are gardeners who head home after a plant-shopping expedition knowing exactly where their purchases will go. I'm usually not one of those people. If I see a plant I want but have no idea where it will live, I buy it anyway—knowing there's always a container. I like to think these plants are in a holding pattern: "Hang out for a while until I find your forever home." Sometimes I know exactly where they'll end up, but the current resident needs to be moved first, so they wait. When the gorgeous *Schefflera delavayi* first hit the market and was quite hard to find, I chanced upon one for a great price. I couldn't pass it up, seeing it as a one-time opportunity. Of course, there wasn't a place in the garden for it, so I stuck it in a large pot. Almost 10 years later, it's still in that same container sitting on my patio. It turns out that pot was the place where it belonged.

A pot can be a sneaky way to fit a new plant into a tight spot where it's not possible to dig in the ground without disturbing the roots of surrounding plants. Just choose a pot with a small footprint and drop it into the planting bed. Or maybe a plant needs a little extra height—a pot placed among plants in the ground slightly elevates it so it can be better seen. Additional height can be achieved by placing the pot on a base; hidden and unseen, or decorative.

Containers also provide the perfect place to experiment with a new plant before committing actual garden real estate. Sometimes a plant is so new to the market, you're not sure how it will perform through the seasons. Is the fall color on that new tree a knockout, or kinda "meh"? Don't dig the hole until you know for sure! Similarly, a short stay in a container is a great way of growing a small plant to a larger size before putting it in the ground.

A dark bromeliad (*Neoregelia* species) and *Tradescantia pallida* 'Purple Heart' are tucked into the top of a tall, slender container in the Portland garden of Lance Wright.

On the flip side, containers are an ideal way to contain a rambunctious plant, one that is only too eager to conquer your entire property if set free in garden soil. The list is long, but a few I've grown this way include various mints, such as *Mentha ×gracilis*, *Equisetum hyemale* (horsetail), and several bamboos. A warning though: anyone planting bamboo in a container should be prepared to keep it well watered and fertilized, and be aware of the long-term implications. Someday that bamboo will want to get out of the container, and what bamboo wants, it often gets. I've heard stories of it busting through cement walls.

Added color and art

After surveying my garden and finding it completely lacking in garden art, an observant visitor declared that my containers brought color to the garden in much the same way artwork might in another person's garden. I had to admit she had a point; by using colorful containers I'd unintentionally added functional art to my garden.

Craig Quirk and Larry Neill, the creative pair behind the Portland garden known as Floramagoria, use pots that are both art and container, such as artist James DeRosso's creative monster pots. They also manage to make their greenhouse look like an outdoor theater, artfully staged with containers and plants. Often a greenhouse sits empty over the summer months, an unused and uninspired space—but not in this garden.

A large container—frequently in a bold color—provides a compelling focal point where paths cross or a sightline ends. For those with restraint, a container left empty adds a touch of drama. However, a container can be just as theatrical planted up, while also satisfying the gardener's need to fill every available inch with plants.

Containers placed on a pedestal or plinth naturally call attention to the plant featured within, as though they're screaming, "Look at me, I'm special!" This is a great way to display a prized specimen or something that might be missed or overwhelmed if planted in the ground.

Water, bog, or vegetable garden

For those who can't or don't want to dig a hole in the ground, a watertight container is the perfect way to create a small water garden. The possibilities are endless as far as the type of container to use: it can be as small as a bowl, or as large as a galvanized stock tank. Most

Clockwise from top left:

Pots in bright shades and boldly patterned foliage add an artful touch to my garden in lieu of actual garden art.

A monster pot filled with carnivorous *Sarracenia* species pitchers must be very scary for the insects in the Floramagoria garden.

Craig Quirk and Larry Neill fill their greenhouse with colorful plants and creative containers, even in the summertime.

Filled with the bold foliage of *Melianthus major* and the orange-red flowers of *Begonia boliviensis* 'Bonfire', a large container adds a dramatic touch where pathways converge in Portland's Floramagoria garden.

A tall red pot stands empty in the Portland garden of John Kuzma and Kathleen Halme.

water plants are sun lovers, a fact I became aware of after placing my first stock tank water garden in the shade. Using a container to grow these plants means you can place it wherever you'll get enough light—four to six hours of full sun—to have blooming water lilies all summer long if that's your desire. Oh, and fair warning. You know the cliché about no matter how big your greenhouse, you'll wish it was bigger? That applies to a water garden as well.

Every water garden is a unique ecosystem. You may want to introduce fish or tadpoles to the mix, or discover you need to deal with algae. I've found consulting a nursery that specializes in water gardens to be especially valuable. When it comes to dealing with algae, the right answer isn't always a chemical one—the correct mix of plants can solve most issues.

Left: *Nymphaea* 'Marliacea Chromatella' (hardy water lily) blooms in my stock tank pond. *Cyperus alternifolius* (umbrella papyrus) and *Thalia dealbata* (hardy water canna) add height, while duckweed shades the water.

Right: An old English livestock feeding trough converted into a simple water feature works well in Gillian Mathews' Seattle garden.

I use these driveway containers as a vegetable garden. There are lemon cucumbers, three different kinds of tomatoes, and of course, basil.

Another terrific use for a watertight container is as a bog garden. There are many plants that appreciate soil that never completely dries out, but don't want to be fully submerged in water. The carnivorous sarracenia and the massive, prehistoric-looking gunnera are two that come to mind.

Large containers make great vegetable gardens because the soil mix and moisture are much easier to control than with in-ground plantings. The soil warms earlier in the spring, but it does dry out faster on a hot summer day. Vegetables need six to eight hours of sunshine a day to produce—there's no way around that—and with containers, you're able to place them perfectly to satisfy this requirement. Containers on wheels can be moved with the sun, to guarantee needed exposure. Older gardeners or those with limited mobility also benefit from vegetable gardening in containers, as there's no need to get down on the ground and back up again.

Fern table or flat-surface planting

Like crevice gardens, fern tables have surged in popularity in recent years. Fern tables elevate horizontal planting surfaces, bringing small plants up close where you can more easily appreciate the details of their foliage and flowers. The best fern tables I've seen include more plants per square inch than would be planted in a traditional in-ground garden planting. In other words, they're cramscaped! Several Pacific Northwest nurseries include fern tables as part of their display gardens; these are typically constructed on a concrete slab set atop concrete blocks. The plantings include a mix of evergreens and small herbaceous plants that die back over the cold months, along with a few spring-blooming bulbs and of course, ferns. I love tracking the seasonal changes of the

Left: A fern table at Joy Creek Nursery in Scappoose, Oregon. It was assembled on a concrete slab which was then set atop a decorative base.

Right: An assortment of stock tanks and other containers in a shady corner of my garden. Flat surface plantings include bromeliads planted in shallow metal trash can lids (placed on cylinders of galvanized ducting) and a fern table on a concrete slab which is resting on another piece of metal ducting.

table plantings when visiting these nurseries. Who wouldn't want year-round interest like that in their own garden? .

Fern table plantings can be created on any raised surface. In *Gardening on Pavement, Tables, and Hard Surfaces*, author George Schenk shows how to plant on wooden, glass, and metal tables, as well as slabs of stone and rock. The assembly process involves mounding piles of soil on the flat surface using rocks and bits of wood to help contain and sculpt the mix. Into the soil go ferns and other shade lovers with pieces of moss tucked in here and there. The final result is a type of woodland setting in miniature. Online, you'll find many tutorials that demonstrate how to build a fern table; the only limit to what you create is your imagination.

While the fern table is perhaps the most popular example of a table planting, this style of gardening isn't limited to shade-loving plants. Why not plant a sun-loving, desert-style table with small xeric plants? As with most container gardens, this enables you to enjoy a small garden in a place that may not otherwise be conducive to planting. My original fern table is located in the dry shade of a neighbor's tall conifer. I can't get a shovel to pierce the ground, and even if I could, the tree's roots suck all the moisture from the soil, making it inhospitable to most plants.

WHAT IS A XERIC PLANT?

Xeric is derived from the Greek word for "dry." A plant described as xeric is adapted to dry conditions and requires little to no supplemental water during the growing season. A xeric landscape is one that receives minimal irrigation. Other words used to describe such plants are "waterwise" and "drought-tolerant." A garden full of xeric plants is often referred to as a "dry garden."

Pots can be made from anything

Some of the most interesting containers I've seen weren't actually designed to hold a plant. They were pie plates, pipes, vents or even trash can lids—and those are just ones I've used in my own garden. If it can hold soil, it can be a container. Ingenious friends have used old laundry sinks, file cabinets, metal bins, sections of rain gutter and culverts, and cast-off kitchen colanders—those colanders provide great drainage. Where do you find these things? Everywhere! Most cities have shops that specialize in recycling and reusing building materials; these are great places to visit. Thrift shops are also a great resource, as well as metal scrapyards and tag sales.

Containers as a Summer Strategy

The decorative and creative aspects are reason enough to plant in pots, but they're not the primary reason I'm hooked. It's the fact I can't stop buying plants that aren't hardy in my climate. I'm not referring to the ones on the edge, but rather plants that don't have the slightest chance of overwintering in my zone 8, winter-wet garden. These tender beauties vacation outside for the summer, then move under cover for winter—the Great Migration. Is it a lot of work? You bet. But thus far it's been worth it, aching back and all.

My version of the Great Migration typically happens in two stages, beginning with the plants that are not temperature hardy, like *Agave attenuata*, *Euphorbia tirucalli* 'Sticks on Fire', and *Aloe dorotheae*. Sometime in mid-October, before our seasonal rains begin in earnest, I start schlepping containers down to the basement, where they'll spend several months hunkered down under lights. My time frame may seem early, given the average frost date in my

At Floramagoria, sections of metal pipe are planted with an assortment of succulents.

area isn't until late November, but it's not the cold that spurs me to action, it's the rain. Rain-drenched soil is heavy, much heavier than the same amount of dry soil. Who wants to haul a heavy container? Of equal consideration is the fact that xeric plants in saturated soil aren't living their best life. By bringing them in while they're still dry, I give them a much better chance of overwintering successfully. Many succulents go dormant, fully or partially, over the

Containers as a Summer Strategy

winter months, so they require minimal water. It may sound harsh, but most of these plants receive water only once—or not at all—the entire time they're indoors. They don't need intense light, either, since they're not actively growing. There are a few succulents that don't go dormant over the winter months—aloes and aeoniums, for example. These need better lighting conditions so they don't stretch and become etiolated (pale and unhealthy), and they may require a little extra water.

The second group that comes into the basement is my bromeliad collection. The bromeliads require bright light, and they definitely don't enjoy the dry air inside the house. A humidifier would be a great addition, but for now I mist the bromeliads several times a week and make sure there is water in the cup formed by their leaves. In addition to misting, the tillandsias—they're bromeliads

Left: Many of my plants in containers spend winter indoors. I jokingly refer to these non-hardy characters as my prisoners. I do my best to keep them happy.

Right: The indoor area devoted to overwintering bromeliad prisoners continues to expand. I'm sure I'll run out of space someday, but so far, so good.

too—get an every-other-week soak in the sink, and then they're laid upside down to dry before being rehung or placed. Since houseplants are experiencing a resurgence in popularity, I feel almost trendy when caring for my wintertime prisoners. I sometimes "shop" among my plants—like going to a houseplant store, only it requires no cash because I'm picking through plants I already own—and rotate them through our upstairs living space. In addition, basement laundry duty is a lot more pleasurable when surrounded by plants.

There is a downside to moving container plants indoors for several months; their leaves acclimate to the lower light conditions. When it's time to reintroduce them to the outdoors, they need to be protected from full-strength sunshine so their leaves don't burn. Even agaves, aloes, and other succulents—plants that love full sun—can't take it right away. Ideally, they'd be placed in a spot that receives only dappled light, or a brief bit of full sun. Once they've had a few days to acclimate, I slowly move them into full sun. If an interim location isn't an option, I've been known to use frost cloth to cover them for a few hours a day, as they adjust. Another good solution is to move them outdoors when the weather forecast calls for extended periods of overcast skies. Inevitably, though, I manage to burn the leaves on at least one plant every year. With time they outgrow it, putting out new leaves that hide the damage, but it still hurts.

The second half of the Great Migration involves moving plants that are temperature hardy but want to stay dry—like the many containerized agaves—into my shade pavilion greenhouse. I have a greenhouse? Yes, for part of the year. As much as I would love a dedicated greenhouse, it's simply not feasible in my small garden, where every square foot has to perform year round. Faced with a wife who kept accumulating containers that needed to stay dry,

my husband came up with a structure that does double duty. In the summertime, it acts as a shade pavilion—a cool, out-of-the-sun place to read on a hot afternoon. In the wintertime, it gets enclosed and becomes a greenhouse, keeping plants dry and out of the wind. On exceptionally cold nights I turn on an electric heater to keep the damaging cold at bay.

The structure's design has gone through several iterations. The current version involves double-sided polycarbonate panels, with air pockets between the two walls, which really helps moderate temperature variance. The walls, ceiling, and doors of this temporary greenhouse slip into place, using the existing structure's framework; during the summer months there's nothing that reveals this is anything but a summer-use structure.

It's a bit of an untruth to say that everything in the shade pavilion green-house needs to stay dry. As plant collectors tend to do, I've accumulated a few thirsty things that go in there just to stay a little warmer on a cold night. It seems obvious, but I've finally learned to group the sheltered plants by their watering needs. Things like *Sonchus canariensis* (tree dandelion), borderline-hardy *Pseudopanax laetus,* and newly purchased plants in nursery pots are placed near the door, where I have easy access to them. The desert dwellers are often out of reach and untouched for the entire winter, and they couldn't care less.

A third, smaller group of containers spend most of the winter months outdoors and are moved into the basement for as long as needed when cold temperatures are in the forecast. These plants, including the tree ferns *Cyathea cooperi* 'Brentwood' and *Dicksonia antarctica,* need the air movement and moisture conditions found outside to stay happy. When I've tried bringing them indoors for an extended period of time, they show their unhappiness with drying fronds, dropped leaves and, in a couple of unfortunate cases, by up and dying.

A SUMMER CONTAINER DISPLAY

Collector and display artist Beth Winter has been accumulating interesting pots, and plants to put in them, for 25 years. She got her start as a container gardener in Petaluma, California, where she displayed over 500 pots in all different sizes—the result of renting and not wanting to invest in a property she didn't own. Moving to Beavercreek, Oregon, meant she could spread out and garden in the ground on her own six acres, but she still brought dozens of containers with her. These days, she puts those containers to use in a summer display of succulents: over 100 pots that spend the winter in her greenhouse and vacation in summer on a gravel area made just for them.

Because of the drainage they allow, Beth uses only terra-cotta and cement containers, with a little rusty metal thrown in for fun. Setting up her container display each spring requires a couple of weeks' time. Before moving them into place, she stops to clean up any damage the plants may have suffered over the winter. Then she gives them a good soak—the first water most of them have had for months. Autumn's teardown goes much quicker—just a couple of days—as things are shuttled into the greenhouse, where they'll stay dry over the winter.

Clockwise from top left:

An *Agave ovatifolia* Beth discovered at a yard sale and couldn't pass up.

A pair of *Aloe dorotheae* and a *Kalanchoe thyrsiflora* thrive in a cement pot.

This plethora of pots is just a small fraction of Beth Winter's container collection.

Beth grows succulents in containers because most of them wouldn't survive planted in the ground in her semi-shady, winter-wet, zone 8 garden. She sets the containers on gravel—rather than lawn or soil—to keep the drainage holes from becoming clogged, and because it suits the style of the plants. The same containers sitting in a mown field wouldn't be as visually pleasing. For a uniform look, Beth likes to top-dress her pots with fine gravel, but warns against using pumice for this, as she did one year. Pumice is light, and when sprayed with water it floated right out of the containers, making a huge mess. Other tips from Beth: raise the containers on bricks or pot feet for improved drainage; invest in a good pair of leather gloves; and use a fast-draining potting soil. Most important of all—be prepared for disappointment and death. A large part of gardening is trial and error, so don't be afraid of change.

Over 100 plant-filled pots spend their winters in Beth's bright greenhouse.

GROW THE UNEXPECTED

Drive down any residential street and you'll see front yard plantings that look rather similar: repeating shade trees and foundation shrubs; lawns that are uniformly big—or small—and allowed to either go dormant in the summertime or are watered and fertilized into lush green sameness. There's a regional style to most neighborhoods and their gardens. Some of this uniformity is the result of new housing developments using the same selection of plants in every yard.

Later, as neighborhoods become established, plants that are widely available and easy to care for become common and seem to multiply like rabbits. A new plant catches on, and soon every house on the block has the foundation shrub du jour—in my neighborhood, for instance, *Nandina domestica* swept through like wildfire. That isn't to say the old standbys aren't still around. Most of the shrubs found on my street date to the late 1940s and early 1950s when the neighborhood was built. There are numerous brightly flowering rhododendrons and camellias—the latter often pruned into lollipops—along with pairs of *Pieris japonica*. I wonder, why always a pair?

For those who long to garden differently, this sameness can be oppressive. Do you really want to be the one who stands out? Of course you do! Because you are fearless.

Breaking with Tradition

While working in the front garden, I regularly end up chatting with people as they make their way to the park at the end of our street. They predictably ask if I'm from the Southwest, as they scan the garden filled with prickly pear cactus, agaves, yuccas, and other desert-style plants. I guess they can't imagine why else a Pacific Northwest gardener would want all those spiky plants in her garden. They're usually shocked when I answer, nope, I'm from Washington State! If we continue to talk, they'll sometimes pull out paper and a pen, or their smartphone, and make notes of plant names and the nurseries where they can purchase these plants for themselves. Those conversations are fuel for my gardening fire! Gardening in the public eye, especially in a way that is different from the norm, gives you an opportunity to share your passion and get others excited about plants.

Previous: A flowering *Echinocereus* hybrid is tucked in next to an agave, in my front garden.

Sadly, a thirsty lawn is still the default in hot, dry, Davis, California. Daring to be different, Gerhard Bock planted this strip of land outside his fence with a striking assortment of succulents and a palo verde tree, *Parkinsonia* 'Sonoran Emerald'.

If you demonstrate an interest in plants or a garden style not common in your area, you're probably going to hear, "You can't do [grow] that here" from a few people. They may not know better or they might be intimidated by a different way of thinking. Perhaps they tried it once, failed, and gave up. But remember, just because you don't see a plant growing somewhere doesn't mean it won't; maybe it just hasn't been tried yet or grown successfully. I killed more than one agave before I figured out what they needed to thrive in my garden.

Depending on what part of the country you live in, your neighbors may embrace a laissez-faire attitude, or they may look at anything that's different as inherently bad. It takes a great deal more courage to garden with a fearless attitude in a conservative lawn-loving suburb than it does in Berkeley, California, or Portland, Oregon. On the other hand, think of all the potential gardeners you'll inspire with your bold gardening ways!

Breaking with Tradition

Identify What Will Grow in Your Garden

Top: Cactus, agaves, and yuccas announce that mine is not your typical Pacific Northwest front yard.

Bottom: Heather Tucker's front garden leaves no doubt there's a gardener in residence—one who does things a little differently in Portland, Oregon.

Pushing boundaries and growing the unexpected is extremely satisfying when the results are positive. However, when attempts are repeatedly met with failure—dead or underperforming plants—even the most fearless gardeners may question their ability to keep going.

Numerous environmental factors influence what will be successful. Some of those factors you can change, others—like climate—you can't. Every gardener I know is ready and willing to talk about the weather. They can tell you if the season is trending wetter or drier than normal. Are the temperatures unbearably high or oddly cold? Awareness of not just the current weather, but also overall climate (long-term weather) will help identify what plants you should be successful growing. The United States Department of Agriculture's (USDA) Plant Hardiness Zone Map (planthardiness. ars.usda.gov) is the standard for assigning hardiness ratings; it's based on the average annual minimum winter temperature in your area over a number of years. The USDA map contains thirteen zones with a 10-degree F spread. Since it's based on averages, any given year can have higher or lower temperatures than what is listed for your area.

There are other hardiness maps, like the Sunset climate zone maps and the American Horticultural Society Plant Heat-Zone Map, but if you're gardening in the United States, most plant labels list only the USDA zones. Sometimes those labels indicate the high end of the scale—the warmest temperatures a plant is thought to tolerate—but they always state the low end, as a frozen plant is

usually a dead plant. Heat stress can kill over time, but cold damage is much quicker to deal the death blow.

Plants don't read labels, or maybe it's more accurate to say plants can't talk, so they aren't able to tell us low they can go. Hardiness ratings for many of the plants we buy are simply educated guesses based on the experience of nurseries and growers who've trialed them and observed how they've done. Assumptions are made based on similar plants and where plants (or their parents) are found growing in the wild. As my friend Janet Sluis, director of the Sunset Western Garden Collection, points out: there are numerous new plant varieties from frost-free climates being introduced to the market. We assume these plants can't take a frost, but are we right? She also warns, "With so much hybridization going on, you never really know what parental genes (so to speak) are going to come through." It's true, you never really know!

Case in point: I fell hard for an orange passionflower, *Passiflora* 'Sunburst', snatching it up as soon as I laid eyes on it. The nursery had it listed as a zone 10 plant—two zones warmer than my garden— but I was so spellbound that I didn't care. That plant bloomed like crazy its first year in my garden, so when temperatures dropped that autumn I dug it out, potted it up, and put it in the basement, hoping it would overwinter there. Sure enough, when planted out the next spring, it took off as though it had never been on hold. But it gets even better! I must have left a bit of the plant behind when I dug it up, because it also reappeared in its original spot that spring. In fact, it has come back every year since, even surviving temperatures in the teens. Is the plant hardier than its listed zone? Or did I get lucky and happen to plant it in a magical microclimate? Likely a combination of both, as this example shows plant hardiness ratings are not an exact science. Experimenting with what you plant and pushing your USDA zone can yield very exciting, and yes, at times, disappointing results. Remember, killing plants is part of gardening on the fearless side.

It's also worth noting that the reverse can happen. Sometimes those responsible for writing plant labels err on the side of being overly generous when describing the low temperatures a plant will survive. Maybe they're working with inaccurate information, or—possibly—being a little unscrupulous and hoping to sell more plants. Whatever the case, it's best to treat the information on a label as a guideline only, not fact. Talk with like-minded gardeners in your area and compare notes on how borderline plants do in your gardens. Then celebrate your successes and learn from your failures.

Your Garden Is More Than a Number

Learning that my summer-dry/winter-wet Portland garden is in the same USDA zone 8 as a friend's garden in Austin, Texas—where it might rain anytime during the year, if it rains at all—certainly changed how I look at the USDA zones. Many of the plants she grows successfully wouldn't last a single year in my cool, winter-wet garden, and ones that sail through my summers would melt under her ruthless Texas sun, where summer days are typically in the 90s, with extended streaks in the triple digits not unusual. If each of us planted solely based on our zone ratings, and not the actual conditions found in our gardens, we'd both end up with very sad plants. Another shortcoming of the USDA zones is the fact that zone assignments don't take into account details on a neighborhood level, just generally by ZIP code. The same ZIP code can have drastically different topographical features: wind tunnels, elevation drops, and hillside shadows where the winter sun never warms the ground.

Zonal denial and zone pushing

Zonal denial is a concept I enthusiastically embrace. Sean Hogan coined the phrase, and his Cistus Nursery definitely supports this approach. But what exactly is meant by zonal denial? Sean's intent was to encourage gardeners to plant things that naturally want to grow in their climate, but look like they may not—plants that fool the eye and create a style and ambience associated with a warmer, drier, or even wetter place. A few examples from my own zone 8 garden are the trunking *Yucca rostrata* (hardy to zone 5), reminiscent of the desert southwest; *Trachycarpus fortunei*, the windmill palm (zone 7); and the tropical-looking, large-leaf *Schefflera delavayi* (zone 7). These plants have weathered an abundance of rain, several inches of snow and ice, and temperatures in the teens, without the slightest complaint. To look at them, you'd think they must need extra protection to survive, but they're all carefree stalwarts. The schefflera's main grievance is our dry Portland summers, but with a little added water, it does just fine.

Under the Big Top at Cistus Nursery. As the sign says: "The heart of all things Cistus; oddball specimens and collectibles for endless conversation."

There are a few adventurous gardeners who stretch Sean's original concept and use the zonal denial label when attempting to grow plants from milder climates—plants that wouldn't typically survive in the environment they're gardening in. Those folks are indeed denying their zones, but I think it's more accurate to call this style of gardening "zone pushing."

"Marginal" is another term that requires explanation. In some plant literature, marginal refers to a plant's preferred location at the water's edge. These are plants that like things wet, but aren't actually aquatic plants and don't want to be submerged in standing water. I use marginal to mean a plant that's on the edge of being hardy—one that might survive below what its comfort zone is thought to be, if it's grown in a warm microclimate or given a little extra protection when temperatures fall.

Successfully growing plants on the edge of their hardiness capabilities requires looking closely at your garden and identifying its unique features. These are characteristics that help you take advantage of everything the site has to offer and grow things just a little outside usual parameters. By utilizing this bag of tricks, zone pushers pull off a little garden magic, and who wouldn't be delighted with that?

Working with microclimates

The magical microclimate I referred to in my story about the orange passionflower is a patch of soil in front of a single-pane basement window. While my basement is kept cool, it's certainly warmer than the winter air outdoors, and a single pane of glass allows some of that heat to escape. In addition, my house is painted dark brown, with a charcoal-colored foundation. Those dark colors absorb any winter sun and slowly release the heat, creating a slightly warmer microclimate nearby. I wasn't thinking about either of those things when I planted the passionflower or when the house was painted. I got lucky, but these conditions definitely contribute to the plant's success.

Identifying microclimates in your garden is easy if you know what to look for. Cold air is heavier than warm air so it settles in the low spots. It's cooler at the bottom of a slope than at the top. In the northern hemisphere, the ground is typically warmer on the south-facing side of your home and next to buildings. Ground-covering hardscapes, like streets, driveways, and parking lots, create a heat island effect in cities. To a lesser degree, a patio and other stone or cement features do the same within your own garden.

As the angle of the sun drops in autumn, some of your sunny spots may become shadier, meaning the soil will stay cooler in the wintertime. Watch for areas where snow or ice takes longer to melt and avoid planting borderline-hardy plants in those spots.

Trees create several interesting microclimates. A dense summertime tree canopy keeps a garden cooler than the surrounding area. If those trees are deciduous, falling leaves in autumn will allow the sun access to the soil underneath, which warms things up. If overhanging branches are high and evergreen, they will provide a bit of cold-air protection for the plants below. And of course,

Lance Wright takes full advantage of the warm microclimate of his streetside garden in southeast Portland. On a steep slope, he grows *Butia capitata* (jelly palm), *Agave parryi* var. *huachucensis*, and *Beschorneria yuccoides* 'Flamingo Glow'.

trees take up large amounts of water, so the ground underneath a tree will be drier than the surrounding area.

Soil that's continuously drier, or wetter, than the overall garden also creates a type of microclimate, one that can be used to your advantage. Once you've located your gutter downspouts and surveyed for areas of standing water, identifying additional wet spots where the soil holds moisture requires a little digging. There's nothing as telling as grabbing a shovel and going a foot or more down into the soil to find out what's happening at the root level. Spring planting in my garden can be an eye-opener when I think the soil is saturated from winter rain, only to dig a hole and discover everything is bone dry just a few inches below the surface. Discovering dry spots can help you identify the perfect place for a xeric plant in the landscape, whereas a perpetually damp spot means a great location for a moisture lover.

Plus, there was little incentive for the plant's roots to do the hard work of venturing out into the native soil surrounding the planting hole. As a result, the plant failed to become established. I'd wanted to improve things but instead made them worse.

Now when planting, I backfill the hole with native soil and add compost topdressing. Over time, the compost works its way into the ground and improves the condition of all the surrounding soil, not just the planting hole.

If you garden on a slope, you have a natural advantage when it comes to drainage. After a heavy rain, some of the water runs off my slightly sloped front garden instead of pooling and soaking in. I've learned to mimic these conditions when planting agaves and other dry-loving plants around the garden. Rather than digging a hole and planting the crown of the agave level with the surrounding soil, I build the ground up and plant above it. I first loosen any compacted soil in the planting area, then I remove as much of the potting soil around the plant's roots as possible so they'll be in contact with the native soil. I place the agave on the ground instead of in a hole, and I mound native soil and gravel or grit around the roots. Picture an agave sitting on a rocky molehill. Slightly tilting

Left: I took advantage of a fast-draining spot behind our patio retaining wall—the builders back-filled with rocks and concrete chunks—to plant a few agaves, yuccas, cactus, and other dry-loving plants. They're also planted higher than the surrounding soil and mulched with pea gravel.

Right: Determined to keep this *Agave americana* alive, Ryan Miller packed pine needles around the base and crown. The needles provided a little protection from the cold and kept the crown dry.

the plant helps with drainage too, because water will run out of the crown, not pool within it.

The finishing step is to mulch around the agave so the planting mound blends in with the surrounding area instead of standing apart. Gravel mulch is especially nice because you can pile it deep and level things out to avoid the volcano look, without worrying about worsening the drainage.

Winter protection

Unless you're gardening in a frost-free climate, your plants will have to deal with temperatures below freezing and possibly snow and ice. Many factors determine just how damaging a freeze may be. Ideally, there will be several light frost events before a hard freeze. These light frosts help our plants harden off and get their natural protection in place for winter. The length of time the temperatures linger below freezing also plays an important role. When it warms above freezing during the daytime and then cools back down at night, plants experience less damage than during sustained periods in which the garden stays frozen day and night.

There are places in every garden that are naturally warmer than others. Plants under the eaves of the house and next to structures will be more protected than those out in the open. Evergreen tree branches provide overhead protection, and garden debris like fallen leaves can be used to protect borderline-hardy plants. When piled around the base of tender plants, a mulch of leaves or other organic material provides protection during freeze-thaw cycles. Some zone-pushing gardeners use straw piled within a frame erected around their plants, but they must be careful not to introduce rot by making the enclosure airtight and trapping moisture inside. Conifer

branches and needles also make an excellent protective layer and are less likely to be blown away by a strong wind.

When faced with the possibility of plant destruction or death, zone-pushing gardeners come up with all sorts of creative ways to protect their valuable plants. After an atypical freeze wiped out the majority of Ruth Bancroft's newly planted garden, she designed individual covers of wood and plastic sheeting—mini-greenhouses—to protect vulnerable plants. My first visit to her garden was early in the spring when freezing temperatures remained a possibility, and a few of these covers were still in place. At first, I was taken aback—I was there to see the plants, not the covers. Then I realized that this was a learning opportunity, and paid special attention to Ruth's approach to protection.

The subject of whether or not to build winter covers for tender plants is one that has been hotly debated. Some feel that if heroic efforts are required to get a plant through challenging weather, then don't bother with it in the first place. We garden to see plants, not plastic. My position is that I don't want to see plastic for the entire winter, but if it protects the plant for a short duration—an arctic blast, for example—then why not? This same reasoning explains why I'm okay with permanent winter covers in

Left: Winter protection for vulnerable plants at the Ruth Bancroft Garden includes mini-greenhouses of wood and plastic sheeting.

Right: In a bad winter storm, one of my *Agave ovatifolia* 'Frosty Blue' plants was wrapped in frost cloth and sat snug under its own little roof.

Portland succulent collector Doug Norseth takes my PVC frame design a step further and builds large versions to cover both in-ground plantings and some of his containers.

out-of-the-way parts of my garden. If the neighbors and I can't see them, what does it matter that they're there?

For short cold blasts, frost cloth, also known as garden fleece or Reemay, is a blessing. It's light, breathable, and designed to trap heat. As a result, it keeps plants a few degrees warmer. It's also easy to use. Just cut and tuck around the plant. If a mix of wet, sloppy snow and freezing rain is predicted, I'll use frost cloth to cover my agaves and tender plants. During one particularly challenging forecast—calling for record-breaking snow of up to 14 inches—my husband quickly fashioned covers from clear corrugated plastic panels, PVC, and bamboo. Simple and inexpensive, these added a layer of protection against a heavy snow load and the rain that usually follows when the temperature warms up again.

HOW TO BUILD A PVC FRAME FOR WINTER PROTECTION

THERE'S A BIT OF MATH INVOLVED IN THIS PROJECT, BUT IT'S STILL PRETTY SIMPLE.

1 Before heading to the hardware store, measure the height and width of what you're covering. I'm protecting a containerized *Agave* 'Sharkskin'. The tip of its tallest spike measures 41 inches, and it is 35 inches wide, spike tip to spike tip. If this were a soft plant, I'd stick close to those measurements. However, I've learned from experience that when an agave is involved, you'll want to add a few inches to the measured width, so the plastic cover doesn't get hung up on a spike and rip. I'm aiming for a frame that's 42 inches tall and 38 inches square. These measurements may increase slightly in the finished product because of the connector pieces.

2 Any good-size hardware store will have a selection of PVC pipe and fittings. I've always worked with half-inch PVC. The pipe typically comes in pieces that are 10 feet long, too long to get home in my car. Luckily, most stores have PVC cutters available and sometimes even staff willing to do the cutting, although the cutters aren't difficult to use if you need to do it yourself. Here's where the math comes in. I need four pieces that are 42 inches for the legs, and four that are 19 inches (half of my 38-inch width measurement). The pipe is 120 inches so, unfortunately, there will be some waste no matter how I cut it. Luckily, PVC is cheap, and you'll probably find uses for the extra pieces. You also need one cross fitting (it looks like a plus sign: +) for the top center (to connect those 19-inch pieces) and four 90-degree elbows. If your store has half-inch PVC snap clamps, grab four of those as well; they'll hold the plastic cover in place. If not, you can order them online, or simply use large binder clips.

3 Now the fun part! Insert the four 19-inch pieces into the + crosspiece and put an elbow on the opposite end of each. Insert the 42-inch pieces into the other side of the elbow, and your structure's frame is complete. If you wanted to make it permanent, you could glue the pieces together. Personally, I like to be able to take the frame apart and store it for the summer.

4 Finally, cover the structure with a large piece of plastic. I typically use an old shower curtain, but if I don't have one on hand, I buy a cheap shower curtain liner. To avoid leaf burn, use a frosted or white piece of plastic, never clear. Center the plastic over the top crosspiece, secure the sides with a clamp or binder clip while tucking the extra plastic to the inside, like folding a sheet at the foot of a bed. If you have extra plastic below the clamp (it will depend on the size of your structure and plastic), cut it off with sharp scissors. That's it!

Project complete! My *Agave* 'Shark-skin' will stay dry over a wet winter un tder its own PVC and plastic cover. This saves having to move a heavy pot and viciously spiky plant.

Top: *Pseudopanax crassifolius* and *P. ferox* outside the Amazon Spheres are stylishly protected from winter cold and snow with custom tents of bamboo and burlap.

Bottom: Preparing for an extreme winter event, the Amazon gardeners wrapped the trunks of *Dicksonia antarctica* (tree fern) in bubble wrap and then burlap, even covering the crown to keep out snow and ice.

For large pots that are too heavy to move under cover but that I want to keep dry, I've devised an individual frame built from PVC pipe. The frame requires no hardware. PVC can be cut to your measurements at the hardware store and fit into premade connecting pieces. Once constructed, I cover the PVC frame with plastic sheeting. I keep these in place during the wet months; they're easy to lift off for airflow on sunny, dry days. As your plants grow you can switch out lengths of pipe to make the cover taller or wider.

Burlap is another material commonly used to cover and protect plants. Martha Stewart wraps her evergreen shrubs and hedges in burlap. The covering protects the foliage from windburn and keeps branches from breaking and splaying out under a heavy snow load.

A word of warning: bubble wrap and other plastic coverings should be used with caution since they trap moisture and can cause damage if allowed to come in direct contact with plant tissue. On a sunny day, plastic can heat up like a small greenhouse and damage plants with excessive heat and sunburn.

ONLINE ADVICE: PROCEED WITH CAUTION

Social media platforms can be a great place to share your gardening successes and failures, to gather inspiration, and to get help with identification of an unknown plant. Social media is, however, not always the best place to get gardening advice specific to your conditions. Not all online platforms are created equal, and while I firmly believe blogs are a great source of information, I've found sites that are heavy on photo sharing and light on text to be problematic. There are many well-meaning individuals who can't help but comment with a bit of instruction or a cautionary tale, even when you haven't asked for it. Plant people are kind and generous; I know they mean well, but it's likely they garden in a vastly different climate or don't even have the same plant. Therefore, err on the side of caution and take that quickly shared online advice with a grain of salt.

HARDY PLANT CHOICES & FOOL-THE-EYE ALTERNATIVES

I live in one of the best gardening climates in the country, so why do I insist on making it difficult by lusting after plants not happy in my area? We gardeners always seem to want what we cannot easily have. I have friends in Southern California who yearn for tulips and peonies, while I'm pining for their South African leucadendrons and the ability to grow tender succulents in the ground.

Since my zone reality is decidedly cooler than my zone identity, I've amassed a garden full of surprisingly hardy versions of what I yearn for, as well as look-alikes: plants that feed my zonal denial by looking like they should not easily grow here. The following are some of the workhorses in my garden that I think you should know about. I've included the generally agreed-upon hardiness zones with plant name—while you'll no doubt want to test (aka push) some of these ratings in your own garden, they're at least a good baseline to start with.

Plants That Look like They Belong in the Desert

Agaves, opuntias, yuccas, aloes, and more—the list is long of desert plants that those of us in cooler climates can grow. There are two requirements these plants have that are nonnegotiable: sun and good drainage. This may seem obvious, but just to be safe I'm saying it. Delve into any list of hardy agaves and you'll find there are several species that can withstand cold temperatures without a problem. What they don't like is the combination of cold and wet—exactly the winter conditions in my garden. Through research and plenty of trial and error, I've ended up with quite a few plants that manage to push through those conditions and live on; some are even thriving.

Agave 'Baccarat' is reportedly hardy to upper zone 7. This stunning gray-green agave was indeed named for the cut crystal, Baccarat, because of the bud imprints on the leaves. I love the bold spikes and the strong overall shape of the plant.

Left: *Agave* 'Mateo' is on the left (its subtle stripe barely visible); *A. bracteosa* on the right.

Right: *Agave ovatifolia*, seen here through the foliage of *Leucadendron argenteum* (silver tree)—in John Kuzma and Kathleen Halme's Portland garden.

Agave bracteosa (squid agave) is favored by many because it doesn't have the traditional agave spikes. It's a gentle agave, but I adore it anyway. It is an easy one to grow and the way the leaves curl does have a certain squid-like appearance. *Agave bracteosa* is hardy to zone 7.

Agave 'Mateo' is another I've had success with. It's the offspring of *A. bracteosa* and possibly *A. lophantha*. 'Mateo' has the curvy leaves of *A. bracteosa*, with the added appeal of a center stripe of lighter green. Sources differ on its exact hardiness (zone 7 or 8), but it's breezed through several cold winters in my garden.

Agave ovatifolia and *A. ovatifolia* 'Frosty Blue' have well-deserved reputations as being bullet-proof. This species is solitary, so it doesn't become crowded by babies at its feet (no free plants, but no wounds from trying to remove them, either). 'Frosty Blue' is a standout for its icy blue coloring. This one is hardy to zone 7 and doesn't seem fazed by a little winter moisture.

Agave parryi is a classic, commonly known as the artichoke agave because its shape is reminiscent of the vegetable. I try to purchase the 'J.C. Raulston' clone; according to Plant Delights Nursery,

it is "particularly well-adapted to winters in wet, humid climates." *Agave parryi* is hardy to zone 7, although some sources go as low as zone 6. In my experience, the variety *A. parryi* var. *couesii* is also well adapted to cooler, wetter gardens; it has longer leaves and is less similar to an artichoke.

Other choice agaves for those in cool, wet climates include *Agave havardiana*, *A. montana*, and *A. neomexicana*.

Opuntias go by many names: prickly pear, paddle cactus, Mickey Mouse cactus. Whatever common name you prefer, opuntias are instantly recognizable as a cactus. According to the U.S. Department of Agriculture, there are opuntias native to all the contiguous United States except Vermont, New Hampshire, and Maine. The opuntia species I've been most successful with is a pass-along plant from a neighbor. I saw it growing in her garden, and when a few pads broke off she allowed me to take them. Her plants came to Portland from the Midwest, via a move, and she has no idea what species they are. I mention this as a reminder that one of the best

Left to right:

Agave parryi 'J.C. Raulston' works well in my climate.

Agave montana sends up its big (life-ending) bloom-spike, in Lance Wright's Portland hellstrip.

Opuntia humifusa, with flowers almost as large as the plant itself.

ways to identify what will grow successfully in your garden is to observe what's growing in gardens in your neighborhood. Then be like Ganna Walska—stroll right up to the front door and ask them if you can have a piece of their plant!

Some of the opuntias I grow include *Opuntia humifusa*, which also goes by the names Eastern prickly pear and Indian fig; *O. basilaris*, the beavertail cactus; *O. cacanapa* 'Ellisiana', a spineless form; and *O. erinacea*, which has such a long list of common names I don't even know where to start. I will point out that while none of these earned their places in my garden specifically because of their flowers, it's always a happy day when they bloom.`

Yuccas seem to be the Rodney Dangerfield of the xeric garden: they get no respect. Many people take the common *Yucca filamentosa*—aka the plant you tried to get rid of but it kept coming back—to represent the entire genus. Yet there are actually over 45 different species, several of them garden-worthy gems. Actually, I like the common *Y. filamentosa* too, especially since it reliably sends up exotic-looking flower spikes each year. The trick is to cut back the plant after it flowers, as that particular section will die. Since this yucca offsets freely, there will be babies to take its place. By thinning out the dying parts you keep the clump smaller and tidy.

Yucca rostrata and *Y. rostrata* 'Sapphire Skies' top my list of must-have yuccas. This architectural trunking species looks far less hardy than it actually is, withstanding temperatures in my garden in the mid-teens. It also grows at the Denver Botanic Gardens in Colorado, which falls squarely in zone 5. 'Sapphire Skies' has especially blue leaves with a thin green edge that glows when illuminated by the sun.

Other yuccas worth seeking out include *Yucca aloifolia*, *Y. desmetiana* 'Blue Boy', *Y. linearifolia*, *Y. whipplei*, *Y. recurvifolia* 'Margaritaville', and *Y. schottii* 'Chiricahua High'.

Unfortunately, there aren't many aloes able to survive freezing temperatures, so their use is limited in a zonal denial garden. *Aloe striatula*, now *Aloiampelos striatula*, and *Aloe aristata*, now *Aristaloe aristata*, are the two exceptions with which I've been successful. *Aloiampelos striatula* can form a tall (to three feet) clump and blooms with bright yellow-orange flowers that are unmistakably aloe-like. Hardy to zone 8, *A. striatula* can die back to the ground and resprout when temperatures warm.

Above: This backlit *Dasylirion wheeleri* is at Joy Creek Nursery.

Opposite top: A patch of *Aloiampelos striatula* blooms at the Point Defiance Zoo & Aquarium (PDZA).

Opposite bottom: A small pair of *Aristaloe aristata*; the red tones are from drought stress.

Depending on which source you refer to, you may find the rosette-forming *Aristaloe aristata* listed as hardy to zone 9, but mine have survived the mid-teens as well as snow and ice. If the forecast looks ugly, I try to protect them with an overturned pot, but I'm not always able to do so. *Aristaloe aristata* can offset to form small clumps, and the tall orange flowers are appealing to humans and hummingbirds. My favorite feature, though, has to be the single filament at the tip of each leaf.

Dasylirion wheeleri, common sotol, is an easy and very spiky addition to the garden. Most sources list it as hardy to zone 6. Small spurs along the leaf margins as well as the frayed fibers at the leaf tips give the plant a somewhat fuzzy appearance when backlit by the sun. It moves like a grass with the slightest breeze.

I've never met an eryngium I didn't like, but *Eryngium agavifolium* is special. Its common name, agave leaf sea holly, says it all: the foliage is reminiscent of an agave. Hardy to zone 6 and tolerant of wet winters, its foliage makes an excellent agave substitute. It also sends up thistle-like blooms that are popular with pollinators.

Hesperaloe parviflora is commonly called the red yucca because of its coral-red flowers and yucca-like leaves. This plant is hardy to zone 6 (some even say 5) and extremely drought tolerant. It does require good drainage and air circulation to prevent crown rot. Hummingbirds love the flowers, which can be increased with generous summer watering.

To my eye, a mature *Nolina hibernica* 'La Siberica' plant appears to be whirling like a child's toy top, looking as though it might just launch into the air. This nolina has a fountain of wide, strappy green leaves, with edges as sharp as razor blades. It's hardy to zone 7 and drought tolerant.

Plants with a Decidedly Tropical Flair

The opposite of the desert garden is the tropical garden, right? Logic says so. In one, you're likely to find dry-loving succulents with plenty of space between each plant. The ground is covered with gravel mulch and spikes abound. The tropical garden contains big leaves practically dripping with moisture; there isn't a bit of open space as plants fill every square inch. These two garden types shall never meet. Wrong! I'm a firm believer in including both styles of planting in your garden if your climate allows for it. Even when it doesn't, you can fool the eye with a few well-chosen imposters. Fearless gardeners find a way.

Tropicalesque plants provide several layers of interest, and examining the different layers is how we'll discuss them: starting with ground covers, moving up to the middle layer of perennials, and then upward again to the large shrubs and trees. While most of these are not truly tropical plants, they have the same qualities: large leaves, bold textures, exotic flowers.

Sedum palmeri (hardy to zone 8, maybe 7) loosely resembles a hardy blue-green aeonium if you squint and use a little imagination. In cool weather, or when water stressed, this sedum takes on a pink blush in my garden. *Sedum confusum* has a similar appearance and hardiness rating but can be a much faster spreader. Some even call it a garden thug, but I've found it easy enough to control—a gentle tug easily removes unwanted plants.

With the common name of cast iron plant, you know *Aspidistra elatior* is tough. This is a large-leaved shade lover. Incredibly slow growing and also available with interesting variegation (spots, stripes, and even stars—again, squint), it is hardy to zone 8 and evergreen.

There are over 100 different ligularias, many of them quite tropical in appearance while also being extremely hardy. *Ligularia dentata* 'Othello' is known for the toothed edges of its large leaves, which start out purplish red but mature to dark green on top with purple underneath. Hardy to zone 4, it dies back to the ground in the fall but is worth finding a shady, moist spot for.

Rodgersia podophylla is another big-leaved perennial that looks right at home in a tropical-feeling garden. Depending on the

Clockwise from top left:

Sedum palmeri, shown here, spreads slower than *S. confusum*.

This *Aspidistra elatior* 'Variegata' is being temporarily grown in a container, while I search for its perfect home.

Ligularia dentata 'Othello' with its spring tinge of purple-red.

Rodgersia podophylla 'Bronze Form' at the PDZA.

form, rodgersia can tolerate temperatures into zones 6, 5, and maybe even 4.

Rare is the plant I praise for its flowers alone, but the pineapple lilies *Eucomis comosa* 'Sparkling Burgundy' and *Eucomis* 'Oakhurst' are just such creatures. The strappy dark foliage adds dramatic color to the garden, but the reason to grow these plants is their tall flower stalks. Often described as something from a Dr. Seuss book, the flowers can reach two feet in height and are topped with a crown of short leaves, like a pineapple (hence the common name). These plants are hardy to zone 7, maybe 6 with protection.

Paris polyphylla (a plant named Paris—what's not to love?) is a perennial that actually hails from China. It resembles a foliage firework with cat whiskers bursting from its center. At least that's what I see. Hardy to zone 5, this one wants a shady spot and requires summer water.

At its most striking when planted en masse, *Mahonia eurybracteata* 'Soft Caress' is known in my house as the palm mahonia. With none of the thorns typical of the North American mahonia, or Oregon grape, and lots of thin, palmlike leaves, this small evergreen shrub is an exotic-looking addition to any garden. Hardy to zone 7 and drought tolerant when established, it has the typical yellow flowers and blue berries of a mahonia.

The podophyllums, or mayapples, are a group of big-leaved herbaceous perennials. While the eastern North American native *Podophyllum peltatum* (zone 4) can go dormant in the heat of the summer, *P. pleianthum* (zone 6) does not, as long as it's given a little water. Other forms with decorative patterns or coloring on their leaves include *P. delavayi*, *P.* 'Spotty Dotty', and *P.* 'Red Panda'.

Plants with a Decidedly Tropical Flair

Rhododendron sinogrande in the
Portland garden of Ann Amato.

Rhododendron 'Ebony Pearl', in
Darcy Daniels' Portland garden.

Rhododendron pachysanthum,
also in Darcy's garden.

Gunnera manicata with its
prehistoric-looking flower cones,
in John Kuzma and Kathleen
Halme's garden.

The red form of *Canna* 'Musifolia',
in Heather Tucker's garden.

Rhododendron is a diverse genus with many more exciting species than the rhododendrons commonly planted. Three of my favorites are *Rhododendron sinogrande*, *R.* 'Ebony Pearl', and *R. pachysanthum*, all selected for their foliage. *Rhododendron sinogrande* (hardy to zone 8) has leaves up to three feet long. *Rhododendron* 'Ebony Pearl' (zone 6) has new growth in shades of red which matures to a dark burgundy-brown, eventually fading to shades of dark green. Some of the leaves also have a bit of a twist to them. The new leaves of *R. pachysanthum* (zone 7) are covered on top with a cinnamon-colored powdery coating (called tomentum by botanists) which fades to a silver-green, while the undersides have a rusty brown coating (indumentum).

Reaching up to 10 feet tall and 14 feet wide, *Gunnera manicata* (zone 7) is not a plant for a small garden, which is why I had to let mine go. If you've got the space and the moisture, then this giant is a spectacular specimen to include, for its big leaves and primordial flower cone.

All canna lilies have a tropical feel. With the largest leaves of them all, *Canna* 'Musifolia' (zone 7) definitely makes a statement. Stalks of the banana canna, as it's commonly known, can reach 12 to 14 feet tall, with leaves up to two feet long.

The hardiest of the bananas, *Musa basjoo* is good to zone 6. For many years, I religiously wrapped the tall pseudostems (a false trunk composed of overlapping leaves) each fall, thinking they needed the extra protection in order to not die back to the ground—until the year I didn't. They did just fine without the wrap, so now I don't bother. If they do die back in colder regions, they'll quickly shoot up from the ground when the weather warms in spring.

Schefflera delavayi is the largest-leaved schefflera that's hardy in my garden (there are several other smaller-leaved species that are equally garden worthy). Its glossy leaves look great year round, but the new spring growth is especially attractive. The flower spikes, which emerge in the fall, aren't what I would call pretty, but they're popular with pollinators. Hardy to zone 7.

Acca sellowiana, pineapple guava, is a seemingly exotic shrub I was surprised to learn would overwinter just fine in my zone 8 garden. The foliage is a deep, dull green with a silver-white underside; the peeling branches have a slight orange tint. Best of all are the blooms: they range from light pink to nearly red in color and are edible—they have a fruity flavor, like bubblegum. Don't eat *all* the flowers, though; leave some for the tasty fruit that follows. Hardy to zone 8.

Many plant snobs turn up their nose at the mere mention of *Fatsia japonica* (zone 7), considering this big-leaf shrub as far too common to include in their gardens. What a lost opportunity! While it's true that Japanese aralia shows up in many commercial landscapes, that's because it's so easy going. For a little extra flair, there is the fabulously variegated *F. japonica* 'Variegata' and *F. polycarpa* 'Needham's Lace' with deeply cut, thinner-lobed leaves.

In gardens where it doesn't die back to the ground each winter, *Tetrapanax papyrifer* can reach tree-like stature and is a must-have for tropical style. With big leaves (to three feet across) on tall stems,

Clockwise from top left:

A large clump of *Musa basjoo* towers over *Hakonechloa macra* 'Aureola' (Japanese forest grass) in the Portland garden known as Floramagoria.

Schefflera delavayi (center) is a standout in my garden.

Acca sellowiana, blooming in June.

The variegated form of *Fatsia japonica* at McMenamins Anderson School in Bothell, Washington.

Clockwise from top left:

Tetrapanax papyrifer can stretch to heights that are common for trees.

Trachycarpus fortunei at the Point Defiance Zoo & Aquarium, in Tacoma, Washington.

My *Trachycarpus wagneriensis*, buried in snow from an unusually wicked January storm.

Eriobotrya japonica with fruit, at McMenamins Kennedy School.

Magnolia macrophylla flowers over a period of several weeks in late May through June.

It may not look it, but *Podocarpus matudae* is a conifer.

rice paper plant is sure to make people stop and stare. In my zone 8 garden, the foliage dies back each year and emerges from the top of the trunks in the spring. In colder climates (to zone 7, perhaps 6 with protection), the entire plant can die back and resprout from the ground.

The windmill palm, *Trachycarpus fortunei*, is a tough-as-nails palm for those gardening in zone 7 and up. Its relative, *T. wagneriensis*, is equally hardy, with slightly more compact fronds, which can give it a tidier look in the garden. Both have hairy trunks, which may be stripped clean for the sake of appearance without affecting its hardiness.

Eriobotrya japonica, the loquat tree, earns a place in my garden for its huge, slightly pleated, leathery leaves (up to a foot in length). The fragrant white flowers in late winter and the possibility of fruit are unexpected bonuses. The tree is hardy to zone 7, but the flowers can be zapped if the temperature drops and the buds freeze.

The bigleaf magnolia, *Magnolia macrophylla*, is truly a sight to see. With giant leaves up to two and a half feet long and flowers up to a foot wide, there is nothing understated about this magnolia. Hardy to zone 5, this tree was one of the very first things I planted in my garden, and I love it more every year. Visitors have a hard time believing it's a magnolia unless they're lucky enough to see it in flower.

How about a conifer that looks tropical? Indeed, *Podocarpus matudae* is just such a creature. There are no needles; instead, you'll see slightly weeping branches with long, wide, bright green, sword-shaped foliage. This yellowwood is hardy to upper zone 7.

Unforgettable Ferns

The ferns suggested here are some of my favorites for adding a lush look to the garden. Planted with the right companion plants, they definitely convey a tropical feel.

The evergreen maidenhair fern, *Adiantum venustum*, is deceptively delicate looking, but once established, this tough character can tolerate zone 5 temperatures and some drought. The arching black stems contrast vividly with the bright green fronds. A slow spreader, it will eventually grow to cover an area about three feet square.

On the flip side, *Onoclea sensibilis*, sensitive fern, definitely earns its common name. Vulnerable to drought, it wants consistently moist soil. At the lightest autumn frost, it browns and calls the season finished. When it's happy, though, it's a beauty. The deeply cut fronds, almost chartreuse in color, are outlined in brown when they first emerge. Hardy to zone 4, sensitive fern is said to spread aggressively in conditions to its liking.

There are many stunning ferns in the genus *Pyrrosia*: *P. hastata*, *P. lingua*, *P. polydactyla*, and *P. sheareri*, just to name four. The pyrrosia ferns all have leathery leaves and most are hardy to zone 7. The many crested, ruffled, and variegated selections provide endless variations. You may need to collect them all—I'm trying to.

Blechnum chilense, the Chilean hard fern, is evergreen in zone 8, possibly dying to the ground in zone 7, but returning from its roots. I've heard some call it the plastic fern because its fronds are so stiff; a more complimentary word would be architectural.

Clockwise from top:

Adiantum venustum (maidenhair fern) is hardier than it looks.

Onoclea sensibilis fronds framed by the leaves of a bromeliad that I dropped into a garden border for the summertime.

Pyrrosia hastata thrives in Lance Wright's Portland garden.

Pyrrosia polydactyla is happy in a shade bowl planting I put together.

Blechnum chilense at the Pacific Connections Garden, part of the Washington Park Arboretum, in Seattle, Washington.

Coniogramme emeiensis 'Golden Zebra' features dramatic yellow variegation on lime-green fronds. It's perfect for brightening up a dark patch of soil. This form of bamboo fern is hardy to zone 7.

Many are surprised by my love of *Matteuccia struthiopteris*, the ostrich fern. Sure, it's common and can be a bit of a thug under the right conditions (moist soil, cool summers). However, when grown in a container—where mine remains a solo act, so far—it can take on proportions similar to a short tree fern, without a trunk. Anything hardy that even slightly resembles a tree fern is a good thing in my eyes. Hardy to zone 3.

Other Plants with Exotic Looks

Following are a few other favorites of mine that look rather lush or exotic—leading people to doubt their hardiness—but are in fact reliably hardy in my zone 8 garden (and even below).

Cold and icy winters have wiped out other astelias, but *Astelia nivicola* 'Red Devil' (zone 7) has not been fazed. I love this plant for its strappy, colorful leaves, which have a bit of metallic shimmer to them.

Echium wildpretii is a remarkable foliage plant I will not be without. Since it's not reliably hardy here (rated zone 9) I plant a couple every spring. If the huge, fuzzy, silver rosette of leaves makes it through the winter, the reward will be a tower of tiny dark pink flowers the following spring, leading to its common name of tower of jewels. While the flowers are a fun bonus, the foliage is the real reason I grow this plant.

Clockwise from top:

Coniogramme emeiensis 'Golden Zebra' boasts signature variegation on its leaves.

Matteuccia struthiopteris may be common, but it still has a place (in a container) in my garden.

Astelia nivicola 'Red Devil' has been hardier for me than other astelias.

Despite its tender nature, *Echium wildpretii* is a must-have in my garden.

The foliage of *Eryngium proteiflorum* is fine, but nothing to get excited about. Mexican sea holly is one of those rare plants I grow for the flowers. What makes the blooms so special? They are the most protea-like flowers hardy in zone 8, something you may have guessed from the plant's scientific name. I've found this one a little difficult to get established, but once it does, it seems just as tough as other eryngiums.

Symphytum × uplandicum 'Axminster Gold', variegated comfrey, is a big-leafed textural addition to the garden, hardy to zone 4. Some say comfrey can be a little on the invasive side, but after four years I haven't noticed a problem—maybe because it gets less water in my garden than it needs to be really happy. This one flowers in the spring and since it's another pollinator pleaser, I let the flower spike stay until the blooms start to fade. That's when I cut it back. As a result of the chop, the plant increases its production of those large leaves.

Every visit I make to Southern California has me lusting after the many proteaceous plants (members of the Protea family) that grow effortlessly there. Thankfully, there are several choice grevilleas (*Grevillea* is a genus in the Protea family) that do just fine in zone 8. Among my favorites are *Grevillea × gaudichaudii*, *G. rivularis*, and *G. miqueliana*. The foliage on these three is extremely varied—from oakleaf shaped, to sharp ferny needles, to fairly large, soft, bright green ovals, respectively. More important, all feature a variation of the curious spider/shrimp/toothbrush blooms.

A small shrub from Tasmania, *Lomatia tinctoria* has fernlike foliage and white flowers which are said to resemble guitars—hence its common name, guitar plant. Another plant in the Protea family, this one is hardy to zone 7.

Clockwise from top left:

Eryngium proteiflorum blooms in Anna Kullgren's Portland garden.

Symphytum × uplandicum 'Axminster Gold' adds colorful texture to the garden at McMenamins Anderson School.

Grevillea × gaudichaudii has oakleaf-shaped foliage.

The leaves of *Grevillea rivularis* are more like needles.

Grevillea miqueliana, with large oval leaves, is not bothered by an early February snow.

Someone saw guitar shapes in the flowers of *Lomatia tinctoria*. Its common name is guitar plant.

Clockwise from top:

Embothrium coccineum blooms
in John Kuzma and Kathleen
Halme's garden.

The flowers of *Callistemon viridiflorus* are stunning, but fleeting.
The seed capsules supply interest
year round.

A stormy sky is the backdrop for
the flowers and emerging foliage
of this *Poncirus trifoliata*.

Embothrium coccineum is commonly called Chilean firebush, after its flaming red flowers. Also from the Protea family, it's a must-have if you are in zones 8–10 (some say 7). Aren't you tempted to grow a plant called firebush? Do it—your hummingbirds will thank you.

I've heard many gardeners from warmer climates dismiss bottlebrush shrubs as common. However, I'm enamored with their exotic flowers and the numerous seed capsules that form after the flowers fade. The green bottlebrush, *Callistemon viridiflorus*, is a unique form with yellow-green flowers and small glossy leaves. It's hardy to zone 7.

For dangerous spikiness, the hardy orange, *Poncirus trifoliata* (syn. *Citrus trifoliata*), zone 5, cannot be beat. Sure, it has pretty white flowers in the spring, and small colorful fruit in the fall, but those long lethal spikes are a year-round treat. *Poncirus trifoliata* 'Flying Dragon' is an especially contorted selection.

INSPIRING GARDEN PROFILES

For this final chapter, I've selected seven gardens to profile—a mix of public and private. They demonstrate the concepts discussed on the previous pages. Taken together, they're meant to challenge assumptions, while inspiring you and your approach to gardening. All of these gardens are firmly rooted in the Pacific Northwest; Washington and Oregon specifically. The gardeners behind these profiled gardens are pushing the envelope of what is expected in this part of the world—pushing themselves to grow things that "shouldn't" grow here.

Previous: Pitchers and flowers of carnivorous *Sarracenia* species, at McMenamins Anderson School in Bothell, Washington.

Yes, I was so excited to be visiting Kew Gardens that I snapped a photo of the Tube station sign.

Travel beyond my home in the Pacific Northwest has deeply influenced my plant lust and my idea of what it means to garden. My own garden would not look like it does if I hadn't spent considerable time in Arizona, California, and New Mexico. I also consider myself extremely lucky to have visited Kew Gardens and the Chelsea Physic Garden in London. In Paris, I saw Parc André Citroën, Jardin du Luxembourg, and Le Jardin des Plantes, just to name a few. Each and every garden we visit shapes the way we think about plants and gardens; seeing these historic sites in Europe was educational, exciting, and humbling.

Through the Garden Bloggers Fling—a yearly meet-up of garden bloggers touring gardens in a host city—I've visited private and public gardens in California, Texas, Colorado, the Washington DC area, and Ontario, Canada. In doing so, I've gained an appreciation for gardening as a regional activity, and what it means to garden in climates drastically different from my own. This garden-focused travel reminds me just how good gardeners in the Pacific Northwest have it. I have immense respect for those of you in parts of the world where the climate is less garden friendly—where frigid winters or blazingly hot summers last for months, or rain is a rare occurrence and not something that can ever be counted on. I hope these profiled gardens and the attitudes of their gardeners speak to you, even if the plant palette may not be directly transferable. On that note, plantsman Riz Reyes acknowledges the amazing range of plants and garden styles available in the Pacific Northwest, but then he goes on to say, "Just because a plant is from the desert doesn't mean it won't grow on the East Coast, in Alaska, or, yes, the Pacific Northwest." He encourages the study of a plant's native growing area and adds, "There is a hardy version or substitute of practically every plant if you look hard enough."

Those wanting to garden outside the lines of what's expected will find a way. I believe the gardeners profiled in this chapter illustrate what it means to garden fearlessly.

The McMenamins Gardens

Gardens around company-owned restaurants and hotels,
located throughout Oregon and Washington. mcmenamins.com

McMenamins is a family-owned hospitality company operating over 50 restaurants, pubs, hotels, and theaters, many housed in refurbished historic buildings. Roughly two-thirds of these properties include plantings—everything from a few containers by the front door to the extensive estate gardens at the 74-acre historic Edgefield property in Troutdale, Oregon.

I'm fortunate to live just blocks from the Kennedy School, a historic elementary school reopened as a McMenamins property in

1997. My development as a gardener was greatly influenced by the gardens around Kennedy School. I was able to discover new-to-me plants, observe their growing conditions, and see how they performed throughout the seasons, all before planting them in my own garden. As a frequent visitor, I got to know the gardeners and didn't hesitate to ask them questions; they were always happy to have a conversation.

To visit a McMenamins garden is to step into a space that feels like a lovingly tended home garden: a little overplanted, a bit wild, slightly exotic. These gardens are cared for by a dedicated garden staff of 17 people, not a quick in-and-out, mow-and-blow crew.

I asked Erich Petschke, corporate gardens manager at McMenamins since 2013, why bother with rare or challenging plants when you could go with the defaults and have a perfectly fine garden? "For the enjoyment and entertainment of our guests," was his response. Although he acknowledged that plants can be a blind spot for many, Erich still feels that all their visitors benefit from the leafy surroundings. He also points out that the McMenamins properties with sizable gardens tend to be ones that function as hotels; the gardens give visitors a sense of place and make McMenamins locations stand out from other hotels in the vicinity.

While you'll see evidence of zone-pushing at McMenamins, the gardeners aren't out wrapping and covering plants when extreme cold hits—there just isn't the manpower for that. Instead, they make educated choices and try to set the plants up for success at the beginning. The gardeners also employ sustainable gardening practices, including pairing the right plants with the prevalent soil conditions in each garden, so there is little need for fertilizing beyond mulching.

All the McMenamins gardeners are encouraged to seek out the "cool" plants and select forms, such as the variegated *Daphniphyllum macropodum*—a rare collector's plant sought by many a

Clockwise from top:

Surrounded on three sides by parking lot, the desert garden at McMenamins Anderson School benefits from the reflected heat.

Tall *Tetrapanax papyrifer* and other mature plantings give a little extra privacy to the guest rooms—former classrooms—along the front of the Kennedy School building.

Yucca aloifolia, *Opuntia cycloides*, and *Nolina hibernica* 'La Siberica', fronted by *Stipa lessingiana* 'Capriccio' in the dry garden at McMenamins Kennedy School.

Lush sidewalk plantings at Kennedy School invite passersby to stop and admire the flora.

plant lover—tucked into a corner at one of their Washington locations. Erich is quick to credit Pacific Northwest plant people and their nurseries—Sean Hogan at Cistus Nursery, Greg Shepherd and Paul Bonine at Xera Plants, and Grace Dinsdale at Blooming Nursery—for the influence they've had on developing the McMenamins style of planting. With so many unique and climate-adapted plants available locally, it's natural that those plants would find their way into the company's gardens.

Both Erich and Riz Reyes, the gardens manager for McMenamins Anderson School in Bothell, Washington, mention overplanting (cramscaping) as a company style. Smart overplanting can be a good "lazy" way to garden, because it keeps the weeds from taking over and helps the soil retain moisture. Of course, part of smart overplanting is knowing when it's time to edit.

Public gardens are a great way for the non-gardening public to gain an appreciation for plants and gardens—go out for dinner, walk through a garden on the way. Since many McMenamins properties are open 365 days a year, winter interest plays a large role in plant selection, and there's something interesting happening in the gardens year round. Through exposure to the plants and gardens at McMenamins locations, visitors will hopefully gain a better understanding of how plants grow together. The meadow garden at Anderson School, for example, is allowed to be natural and a little unkempt. Referred to by many as the pollinator garden because of the buzz and hum of myriad insects, it gives guests the opportunity to witness the chaos and dynamic beauty of meadow ecology.

The opportunity to showcase the diversity of plants we can grow here in the Pacific Northwest is something Riz appreciates. He plants to take full advantage of the broadleaf evergreens, beautiful bark, and textural grasses available, treating flowers as icing on the cake. Speaking of flowers, Riz, who moonlights as a floral designer, does the floral arrangements for the events that take

Clockwise from top left:

Digitalis ferruginea (rusty foxglove) and *Achillea filipendulina* (fern-leaf yarrow), in the meadow garden at Anderson School.

An unidentified *Opuntia* species and *Nassella tenuissima* mix it up at Edgefield.

McMenamins' multilocation gardener Ryan Miller made an impulsive purchase when he found this large *Agave americana*. He knew the chances of it surviving through an average winter were slim, but resolved to go the extra mile when "tucking her in for her winter slumber." Fortunately, the soil on the banks of the Columbia River at the Kalama Harbor Lodge location provides excellent drainage. An agave on the edge of the mighty Columbia—now that's fearless gardening!

Verbena rigida is backed by sharp agave spikes at Anderson School.

The entrance to the vegetable garden and orchard at McMenamins Edgefield is marked by a theatrical red door.

place at Anderson School—using flowers and foliage from the garden and supplementing with purchased stems as needed.

Using what's available in the garden—soil to plate, as Erich refers to it—is a fundamental principle within the organization. Kim Kincaid, head gardener at the Edgefield property, oversees a half acre of vegetable production, most of which is used at the on-site Black Rabbit restaurant. Fruit tree yields include pears, which end up in McMenamins' distillery-made pear brandy, and apples, which the winery uses in several hard cider flavors.

Botanicals such as rose petals become ingredients in spa massage oils and pedicure baths, while at the Anderson School, gift shop visitors can purchase lavender bundles grown on the property. If they visit at the right time of the year—Mother's Day, during the summertime Crackedpots event, or Oktoberfest—guests at Edgefield can even purchase plants divided or propagated from the garden.

Young plant lovers are included in the McMenamins magic. Riz admits to planting things near pathways for kids to discover—interesting treasures meant to capture their imaginations. He also enjoys interacting with adult guests as they pass through the garden, answering questions and, on occasion, organizing Friday afternoon garden tours for both hotel guests and locals. Included in his plant-focused outreach is gently educating the non-gardening staff on the plants growing around them and acting as an advocate for gardeners everywhere. He reminds us that public gardeners are skilled professionals and horticulture should be treated as a viable career option. To preserve our open public spaces, we need future botanists and ecologists.

ADVICE FOR GARDENING FEARLESSLY, FROM THE MCMENAMINS GARDENERS:

- Pick a cool plant, but start small, so you're not experimenting with something expensive (remember, Ruth Bancroft started her garden mostly with plants in four-inch pots).

- Don't plant tiny, untested, or marginal plants in the fall; start those in the spring so they have time to get established. That said, fall is a great time to plant things that are winter hardy in your area.

- Tune in to what speaks to you. If you see a plant you want, don't be discouraged if, at first glance, it doesn't seem like it would work in your garden. Experiment!

- Have an adventurous sense of gardening and remember to use containers. Many newly acquired treasures can be container focal points. Not only can that be a test of hardiness, it also gives you time to decide where the plant's ultimate home in the ground will be.

- The only fear that should exist in gardening is, "Is there enough money in my bank account?"

John Kuzma and Kathleen Halme's Hummingbird Garden

Private garden located in Portland, Oregon

Designed by plantsman Sean Hogan, this garden seamlessly integrates Sean's horticultural vision and knowledge with the plant collecting tendencies of its owners, John Kuzma and Kathleen Halme. I have been fortunate to make at least annual visits to this garden since its beginning and I've watched it evolve much like I have my own garden. John and his wife Kathleen have been very generous in sharing their garden and I hope they won't be surprised to learn that on some level I think of it as my garden, too—my larger garden, the one that I never have to work in, the one I just get to enjoy.

The garden sits on a little less than half an acre in southwest Portland, at 600 feet elevation. Visitors must wonder if they are really still in Oregon, because the garden's plant palette draws from South Africa, Australia, the Mediterranean, China, and the west coast of the United States.

John's interest in gardening began with his love of home-grown tomatoes and the desire to master the art of growing them. He describes his previous Portland garden as more traditional in style. Lurking just under the surface of this staid gardener, however, was an adventurous plant lover ready to embrace a strong new look. John began attending the Northwest Flower and Garden Festival in Seattle and became familiar with the work Dan Hinkley was doing at Heronswood botanical garden. From nursery owner Roger Gossler, John discovered the design work of Glenn Withey and Charles Price, who were major contributors to the original perennial border at the Bellevue Botanical Garden in Bellevue,

Clockwise from top left:

Tall, trunking *Yucca rostrata* specimens are underplanted with younger *Y. rostrata* and *Opuntia aurea* 'Coombe's Winter Glow', in a front corner of the Hummingbird Garden.

Variegated *Daphniphyllum macropodum* offers distinctive foliage.

The pond provides a source of water for the garden's wildlife, including a few marauding raccoons. Thoughtful placement means it's visible from the kitchen window and enjoyed from inside the house as well.

Sean Hogan, the Hummingbird Garden's designer, refers to the large gravel rectangles in the front and back gardens as "enforced negative space" and points out they're designed at a scale that relates to the house, a sort of living room carpet just outside the front and back doors.

One of John's favorite plants in the garden is *Quercus guyavifolia*.

Washington—they drafted the plans for the next iteration of John's garden. In the mid-1990s, Sean Hogan and his late partner, Parker Sanderson, moved back to Portland from the Bay Area and opened Cistus Nursery. John became an early and frequent customer.

When a divorce led him to shop for a new home and garden, John was on the lookout for a flat lot with plenty of sun, where he could indulge his growing lust for sun lovers like agaves and palm trees. John self-identifies as a plant collector and acknowledges that he wasn't sure how to best organize his ever-increasing collection; he knew he needed assistance and had been talking with Sean about a design for the new garden even before purchasing the property. Sean's zonal denial approach was a perfect match, and his extensive use of broadleaf evergreens and Mediterranean plants appealed to John. Part of Sean's design process involves channeling the client and how they will use the space. With a plant lover as a client, Sean says it's largely about editing down plant lists, rather than looking for plants to add.

Sean's design for this garden includes a strong framework of boundaries, negative space, and themed sections within the garden to help direct new plant acquisitions. Once the property's purchase was finalized, the original garden's Japanese maples, morning glory, fruit trees, and lawn were removed to create a blank slate. Planting took place from the fall of 2009 into the spring of 2010.

Asked what the garden would be like if he hadn't worked with Sean, John says, "I don't even want to think about it," adding, "When you have someone like Sean, with his background and perspective, it would be crazy not to work with him." Kathleen takes it a step further: "What would Portland be like without Mount Hood?" she says, a statement acknowledging both Sean's importance to the garden and his status as a gardening icon in the region. John shares that Sean's overall, cohesive design took the anxiety out of creating the garden and making the investment. Sean continues to guide the garden's evolution and sometimes returns when there are open gardens, answering questions and enjoying being in the space he designed with others who may be experiencing its magic for the first time.

John estimates about 80 percent of the garden's plants were selected by Sean; 20 percent by John and Kathleen. He adds that Kathleen has encouraged the addition of color whenever possible. Some of John's favorite selections include two oaks: *Quercus guyavifolia* (an evergreen oak) and *Quercus suber* (cork oak). Flowering perennials and vines, such as *Abutilon* 'Victor Reiter' and *Passiflora* 'Fata Confetto', earn high marks, and the variegated *Daphniphyllum macropodum* gets a thumbs-up as well.

One favorite John thinks maybe underappreciated by fellow gardeners is *Acca sellowiana*, the pineapple guava. It's easygoing and provides so much: evergreen foliage; beautiful, edible flowers; and tasty fruit. John also feels *Alstroemeria* 'Indian Summer' deserves to be more frequently planted; it expands slowly but is not a thug like other alstroemerias, and it's "always" in bloom.

After a particularly bad winter that saw temperatures drop to eight degrees F and created a few holes in the garden, John filled the empty spots with *Salvia darcyi* and *Agastache mexicana* 'Sangria' before a tour group came through. The two plants turned out to be such welcome additions—the hummingbirds love them—that if they don't make it through winters on their own, he replants them each year.

Since adding a greenhouse to the garden, John's overwintering capabilities have increased substantially (not that he's afraid of a little work to get a favored plant through adverse conditions). His *Leucadendron argenteum*—also known as the silver tree, a species in the family Proteaceae—is protected each fall with a double-walled plastic cover and incandescent Christmas tree lights for warmth. The tall bananas (*Musa sikkimensis*) and orange kangaroo paws

(*Anigozanthos* 'Fiery Sunset') get the same treatment—lights and plastic sheeting—which has allowed the kangaroo paws to survive in the ground since John's first buying trip to California in 2011. Taking things a step further, the crevice garden has its own rooflike cover built over it, and the truly tropical plants are lifted, potted up, and moved to the greenhouse.

Gardening with plants on the edge has resulted in a few fatalities, like the loss of several large specimens of *Agave americana* var. *protoamericana* 'Silver Surfer' that turned to stinky mush during a harsh arctic event one winter. John says there's been a steep learning curve involved in figuring out how to care for some of the plants, and he lost a couple of manzanitas (genus *Arctostaphylos*) early on by overwatering them, before he knew better.

Anyone who has ever experienced the challenge of starting a garden on their own, then added a gardening partner to the mix, will find John and Kathleen an inspiration. Kathleen says she was a little "obsessive with order and form" in her previous garden, not surprising for someone who is an accomplished poet. She notes this garden is teaching her new forms of patience, as she adapts to a garden some might see as a little loose and wild. A lover of arisaema, also known as jack-in-the-pulpit or cobra lily, Kathleen is introducing a whole new genus of plants to the garden. Whenever Kathleen makes suggestions for garden additions, John asks himself, "What would Sean say?"

Not surprisingly, John and Kathleen both agree that if she didn't love gardening, they wouldn't be together—gardening is that important in their lives. When she asked what John likes most about plants, he replied, "Watching them change and grow." John sums up the feeling of living in the garden: "Why wouldn't you want this beauty around you every day, rather than going away on vacation to find it?"

John Kuzma and Kathleen Halme's Hummingbird Garden

JOHN'S ADVICE FOR THOSE WANTING TO GARDEN FEARLESSLY:

- Pushing your zone can be overdone; don't tackle more than you can be successful with. Having a greenhouse makes a huge difference.

- A little experimentation can pay huge dividends. Citing *Acacia covenyi*—a small tree with smooth dark stems and silver-blue leaves—as an example, John encourages planting a few things that might be risky. This fast-growing acacia is hardy to 15 degrees F, so gardeners in zone 8 could get several years of enjoyment before cold temperatures cut it down.

- Spend a little more on plants you treat as annuals by using perennials as annuals. Some of John's favorites for this are *Cuphea llavea*, *Leonotis leonurus*, and tender salvias.

- Find trustworthy sources for plants. For the Portland area, John recommends Cistus Nursery, Xera Plants, and Blooming Junction. Other places he shops include Ravenna Gardens in Seattle, and the mail-order nurseries Gossler Farms and Annie's Annuals.

- Thinking about the future and aging, John and Kathleen are looking for ways to reduce the labor involved in gardening. They're not afraid to hire help for some of the big jobs, and John notes that by planting out "annuals" (whether they're true annuals or perennials acting as annuals) in the same spot each year, you don't have to rework the drip irrigation system for new plantings. This saves time and prevents watering mishaps.

Ron McKitrick's Hillside Desert Botanical Gardens

Private garden located in Yakima, Washington. hdbgi.com

Growing up in Washington State, I'm familiar with the stereotypical view that it "rains all the time" there. As with most stereotypes, this one is quickly disproven. Even the "rainy" western side of the state turns dry in the summertime, and the central and eastern parts are dry—some desert-like—year round. Ron McKitrick's Hillside Desert Botanical Gardens is located in Yakima, Washington, where his average annual rainfall is just six to eight inches. The garden isn't typical of what you'd expect to see in this part of the country, with tall *Yucca brevifolia*, spiky *Agave utahensis* var. *nevadensis*, and more *Echinocereus* (hedgehog cactus) hybrids than you'd think possible. Yet Ron has been proving these plants are right at home here since he started planting them in 1982.

Ron grew up on a ranch and fruit orchard in Naches, Washington, eventually heading to school at Washington State University, where he thought he would earn a degree in horticulture and return to take over the ranch. Once at college, however, a friend encouraged him to look into the pharmacy program, saying "pharmaceuticals aren't that far from horticulture." After graduation, Ron became the pharmacist at a Yakima area hospital and stayed there for 48 years. He never lost his interest in horticulture, though, and early on became a collector of houseplants.

In 1976—with houseplants in tow—Ron and his family moved to the home that would become Hillside Desert Botanical Gardens. Ron built a small greenhouse in the backyard for those houseplants—a mix of cactus and common succulents—followed a few years later by a second, larger greenhouse. When the second

Clockwise from top left:

Clockwise from top left:

Ron McKitrick estimates his tallest
Yucca brevifolia (Joshua tree)
at the Desert Hillside Botanical
Gardens is 30 years old.

This impressive crested *Cylin-dropuntia imbricata* grew from
a cutting of a greenhouse plant;
it's one Ron often sells or trades
pieces of. He is meticulous about
removing any non-crested growth.

Ron's greenhouses are chock-full
of potted cactus and succulents;
many vacation outside for the
summer.

Agave utahensis var. *nevadensis*
and an unknown *Cylindropuntia*
hybrid that just appeared—seeded
itself—in the garden around five
years ago.

The southeast side of the house
is where Ron first started experimenting with outdoor plantings.
Initially, he covered the plants with
plastic each winter. Then they got
too large and he discovered they
did fine without protection.

structure filled up, the plants eventually began to move outside, a natural evolution as Ron calls it. He was willing to test things and see what would work. "Nobody else in the area was doing it. Why not?"

Plantings first went against the southeast side of the house, since Ron figured it was the warmest spot on the property. Three years later, he'd covered that entire area and was poised to take over the entire backyard. He started planting small raised sections surrounded by railroad ties—Ron refers to each individual unit as a garden—and added one garden per year, for 20 years. His biggest setback in the garden wasn't plants dying, but rather pipes in the greenhouse freezing, bursting, and causing flooding.

Ron amassed his collection of cactus and succulents by first buying what he could find through local sources. Once he had everything that was available locally, he expanded to mail order. Plants arrived with bare roots, wrapped in newspaper, a couple times a week. In those early days, mail order included a lot of letter writing and waiting. Now Ron acquires plants via the internet and estimates there are currently several hundred different kinds of cactus in the gardens.

Desert Hillside Botanical Gardens is indeed on a hillside. The gardens sit approximately 200 feet higher than the surrounding valley floor. As a result, spring plants in the garden are about two weeks ahead of others in the area. Wintertime lows in Yakima typ-ically fall to between five and ten degrees F, although below zero temperatures do occur. Summertime highs frequently reach into the triple digits. Summer means dry days. Winter and spring are the "wet" season—if you can call it that. The USDA Zone Map puts Yakima in zones 5 and 6, and snow is a fact of life.

When visitors mention seeing snow on saguaro cactus in the Southwest—and hint that perhaps Ron should be growing the des-ert plant icon—he points out how important daytime temperatures are to plant life. In the desert Southwest, things don't stay frozen for long periods of time because temperatures typically climb above freezing during the day. When daytime highs stay below the freezing mark—as they do in Ron's area—that's when damage occurs to vulnerable plant tissues. The saguaro, *Carnegiea gigantea*, can withstand dips down to the teens, but only for brief periods of time.

Asked about growing cactus and agaves, Ron acknowledges that some people are fearful of the spines and worry about children and dogs playing nearby. Then he adds, "They'll follow that ball into the garden just once—one time of messing with the spines, and they'll learn." He goes on to admit he himself has fallen into a cactus more than once. "You pull out the spines and get on with it. . . . Sure, it hurts while you're pulling them out, but quick enough you forget about the pain."

Through opening his garden, lecturing, and giving demonstrations, Ron has become a local celebrity and is often referred to as "the cactus guy." He's happy to help locals and visitors create their own desert gardens, if feasible, and he sells plants he propagated himself.

As for favorites, Ron has a few. "Definitely the Joshua tree, *Yucca brevifolia*, and the echinos, *Echinocereus*, because of their flowers—they spread and they're winter hardy." Ron explains that the *Echinocereus* varieties he grows are different from the ones you see in the Southwest; his have bigger flowers because of their dormancy period in the winter.

Ron says he finds the life cycle of agaves fascinating. By the first week of May, he can tell if there's going to be a bloom. If—by that time—there's no point forming, ready to shoot out of the center of the plant, then it won't be a blooming year. Ron hasn't been able to create any agave hybrids in his garden because he's never had multiple species flowering at the same time, though he does estimate he's had at least 10 different kinds of agaves bloom.

Clockwise from top left:

Ron identifies this as *Echinocereus triglochidiatus* hybrid form, a cross that occurred in the garden.

A small selection of the plants Ron offers for sale.

Agave utahensis var. *nevadensis* sends up a bloom stalk right on Ron's schedule. This photo was taken on May 10.

A wide view of the many plants that make this garden so distinctive. Blooming begins in mid-April but the best bloom time is mid-May through June.

WORDS OF GARDEN WISDOM FROM RON:

- "It's not the fool who makes mistakes, it's the fool who doesn't learn from them."

- When someone voices concern that a particular plant may die, Ron asks, "Does the possibility of getting a flat tire keep you from driving a car?"

- A plant's native range matters. Look to the climate it comes from for clues on whether or not it will grow in your environment. He adds, "Try it and learn, take a cutting first for insurance."

- When planting a new area, be sure to cluster together any of the plants you might need to protect in the winter. Ron still covers some of his and wishes he had grouped them so he'd have a smaller area to protect.

- Ron recommends not pulling a plant out right away, even if it looks dead. It might be fine and make a comeback. Leave it until you're sure it's dead.

- Remember: "What you see are my successes, you don't see my failures—they're in the compost pile."

Felony Flats Botanical Garden

Private garden of Eric Peterson and Robert Brigham, located in Portland,
Oregon

This exotic garden began when the gardeners were only renting their house. Eight years—and many plants—later, they now own it and are quite literally putting down roots. Despite its big-sounding name, Felony Flats Botanic Garden is a small private garden surrounding the home of Eric Peterson and Robert Brigham. The name is a bit of wordplay on the hardscrabble neighborhood that surrounds their home in southeast Portland. After my first visit years ago, I dubbed it the Movable Garden, because most everything was growing in containers—some 170+ of them—many large enough to hold a small human. These numerous containers served two purposes. Most important, they allowed Eric to invest in and surround himself with the plants he loved without the possibility of having to leave them behind when he eventually purchased a home elsewhere and moved. Second, since most of his collection needs winter protection, the containers allowed him to move the plants into a greenhouse when the cold season arrived.

But let's back up. Eric, an Oregon native, moved to the house in 2011 and began removing lawn and invasive plants like *Arum italicum* and thuggish alstroemeria. His partner Robert joined him a year later. Their plant tastes are quite diverse. Eric appreciates dramatic, spiky, architectural plants, while Robert loves old fashioned flowering perennials—"old lady plants" as he calls them. The couple manages to keep their distinct styles separate by working in different parts of the garden: Robert in the front of the house and Eric in the back. That's not to say there isn't some intermingling of plants, but it's a division of space that works for them.

One of Eric's earliest gardening memories is building a greenhouse when he was just a kid. Three attempts and lots of trial and error later, a wood and fiberglass-sheet structure finally held up. A gift of a tropical passionflower from his gardening mother got him headed down the zone-pushing path he still follows today.

Robert got his gardening start growing marigolds in his bedroom when he was a kid, then moving on to do landscape work for his honorary grandma, Billie, on her large parcel of land in California, where he grew up. Grandma Billie gave Robert his first copy of *Sunset Western Garden Book*, the pre-internet plant bible for those gardening in the West—and he was hooked. Raised on a traditional gardening style, Robert initially thought Eric was a messy gardener; plants shouldn't touch and you should be able to see the ground between them. He's come a long way since then.

Measuring just 3900 square feet, Felony Flats Botanical Garden is smaller than the 5000 square foot lot typical for Portland. However, through intensive planting and a layered style, the pair has managed to squeeze in a plant collection worthy of the botanical garden moniker. Eric estimates about two-thirds of his plants are in containers, and more than half were acquired via road trip plant shopping. He thinks nothing of spotting an unusual plant on Craigslist and driving to California to pick it up. A recent buying trip was up to Ellensburg, Washington, where he scored the top of a large, old-fashioned windmill, now anchored to the back of the house.

One of Eric's first garden projects was to convert the home's garage into a greenhouse, done while still renting, with the blessing of his landlord. He tore the structure down to the frame, and on the bottom half put up shingles over the existing shiplap siding. The top part of the walls and ceiling were fitted with salvaged windows from an uncle; other windows were reclaimed from around town. Now that he owns the property, Eric has drawn up detailed plans to rework the building, opening up the garden-facing side

Clockwise from top left:

Eric hunts Craigslist and other online classified ads for distinctive items to add to the garden. These finds are usually plants, but not always. The top of an old-fashioned windmill was one recent purchase.

An *Agave americana* var. *mediopicta* 'Alba' in the front garden, along with *Alstroemeria* Colorita ® 'Louise' and *Sedum erythrostictum* 'Frosty Morn'.

The back garden includes plenty of space for relaxing, with both a dining area and benches near an outdoor fireplace that Eric and Robert built with bricks and stones from free listings on Craigslist.

An assortment of plants hugs the side of the greenhouse, including *Podophyllum pleianthum*, *Aeonium arboreum* 'Zwartkop', and *Araucaria araucana* (monkey puzzle tree).

Tall *Musa basjoo* frame the front door at Felony Flats Botanical Garden. Color comes from potted *Fuchsia* 'Golden Herald' and the big leaves on the left belong to *Brugmansia* 'Golden Lady'.

with double doors, which will make it easier to move plants out and in during the spring and fall migration. A man of many talents, he's making stained glass panels to replace some of the clear glass, so the revamped greenhouse will be a work of art as well as a plant shelter.

The shift in mindset from renting to owning their home has been so redefining for Robert that he compares it to "coming out of the closet all over again." He and Eric have since planted several trees, including freeing a columnar Crimson Spire™ oak, a hybrid between English and white oak, from its confined life in a pot. They also have plans to make several hardscaping changes—a patio instead of gravel in the back garden and a proper front porch—as well as finally installing drip irrigation.

The garden's location on Portland's eastside means they suffer the effect of the harsh winter winds that rush through the Columbia River Gorge, defoliating evergreens and even breaking a pane or two of greenhouse glass. While Robert claims to not have the bandwidth to deal with moving heavy containers in and out of the greenhouse in the spring and fall, it was he who protected the large first-year specimens of *Echium pininana* that punctuate the back garden by throwing an old shower curtain and fleece blanket over them on cold nights. His hope was that they'd live to send up their majestic bloom spike the following spring. They lived, but that bloom didn't happen. Biennials don't always realize they're expected to flower and die in their second year.

Visitors—Eric and Robert have opened the garden for local groups in the past and will again—can expect to see large containers full of flowering brugmansia, trunking *Yucca rostrata*, sizable agaves, aloes, aeoniums, and, if the timing is right, even a "blooming" cycad, perhaps a first in Portland. What they won't see is lawn; why waste the space and resources?

Despite the fact that Portland's climate doesn't support growing citrus, they have a small collection, including the Buddha's hand

Clockwise from top left:

The big floppy leaves of *Echium pininana* are worth the effort to overwinter, even if the plant doesn't reward you with a bloom spike the following spring.

Citrus medica var. *sarcodactylis*, Buddha's hand citron, shows why its common name is appropriate.

The garage-to-greenhouse conversion involved replacing the original car-sized door with French doors.

The giant cone of the cycad *Dioon spinulosum* creates a stunning display.

Potted agaves, including *Agave americana* 'Variegata' and *Agave ovatifolia* at the base of painted statuary in Eric and Robert's garden.

citron, *Citrus medica* var. *sarcodactylis*, in a container. Robert points out that these can be left outdoors for a good part of the winter since they're hardy to zone 10 (they bring them indoors when the temperature drops to the mid-thirties F).

Asked about undervalued plants that more people should be growing, Eric extols the virtues of unusual yuccas like *Yucca rostrata* and *Y. linearifolia*, and cold-hardy agaves such as *Agave ovatifolia* and *A. parryi*. Because they look exotic, people think they're much more difficult to grow than they actually are.

Being active plant collectors with a small garden, the pair is learning to embrace what Robert calls "Phase Two gardening," or heavy editing. Asked for an example, he points to a large edgeworthia (Chinese paper bush). Once upon a time it was a coveted plant they were thrilled to acquire, but they just don't love it anymore, and that's okay. They're eying the space for a small koi pond and looking to rehome the edgeworthia. It's perfectly fine to let a healthy plant go if it's not making you happy any longer.

ADVICE FROM THE OWNERS OF FELONY FLATS BOTANICAL GARDEN:

- Don't let renting stop you from gardening. Gardeners find a way to garden.

- Network in your community and get to know like-minded gardeners—you'll benefit from their support and experience. Join Facebook groups for the type of plants you want to grow, and use social media hashtags (#coldhardycactus, for example) to research and learn.

- Experiment. Remember that trial and error is your best teacher. Don't be afraid to kill plants.

- Gardening can demand large chunks of your time. Don't be afraid to let the house chores slide during gardening season; that's what winter is for.

- Plant things with winter interest, like hellebores, in garden areas you'll pass through year round. Regularly feed plants you rely on for heavy bloom output, especially if they're growing in containers. Miracle-Gro is scorned by many gardeners, but brugmansia, for example, loves the blue stuff.

The Amazon Spheres Neighborhood

Corporate campus and public spaces, located in Seattle, Washington.
seattlespheres.com

It was 2016 when I first became aware of the growing Amazon campus in downtown Seattle. A friend had written a piece about the interesting plants they'd used in the first phase of the development, and I vowed to keep track of the project. Fast forward to February 2018. The Amazon Spheres—three glass-domed conservatories—had just opened, right before hundreds of gardening enthusiasts descended upon Seattle for the Northwest Flower and Garden Festival. Even though the Spheres had nothing to do with the show, they were what everyone was talking about. I took off one afternoon to see them for myself.

Turning a corner and standing in front of the futuristic-style buildings filled with plants was a moment I will never forget. As a plant lover, the pull was intense, but others were stopping to look up too. I don't think it's exaggerating to say we were all in awe. Of course, the feeling was tainted by the realization that I might never step inside one of the orbs—Amazon had yet to launch their public access program—but I soldiered on and was thrilled to discover an equally inspiring collection of plantings at ground level, outside, surrounding the conservatories.

There is a direct relationship between the plants inside the complex and those around it. According to Matthew Wood, principal at Site Workshop—the landscape architecture firm who, along with NBBJ Architects, designed the project—the plantings around the Spheres were intended for the public as a taste of what's inside. Hardier bromeliads like *Fascicularia pitcairnifolia* and *Ochagavia carnea*, which are planted outside, hint at tropical bromeliads, such as *Vriesea saundersii*, inside.

Clockwise from top left:

The Amazon Spheres are three spherical conservatories that are part of Amazon's corporate headquarters in Seattle, Washington.

The living wall at the Spheres is 67 feet tall.

Parahebe olsenii and *Ochagavia carnea* are planted outside the Spheres.

The semi-epiphytic *Medinilla* 'Gregori Hambali', inside the Spheres.

Dicksonia antarctica, the Tasmanian tree fern, is said to be hardy down to the mid-twenties F.

Those traversing the public sidewalks and pathways which cut through the block are surrounded by plants that evoke a feeling of the exotic and unfamiliar, such as a row of tall, lacy tree ferns. Although one of the hardier tree ferns, *Dicksonia antarctica* is not a common sight in the Pacific Northwest. Many scoffed at the idea they'd survive their first winter. Yet they did, and not just a typical Seattle winter, either, but one that brought a lot of wet snow that stuck around far longer than anyone anticipated. Of course, knowing the location's microclimate helped—the tree ferns are still a bit of a gamble, but the heat island of downtown Seattle increases the odds of continued success.

So, what about those Spheres? Why are they part of the Amazon campus? The site's original plan called for additional office buildings. Thankfully, the decision was made to instead create a building inspired by Victorian conservatories—a unique space that would allow employees to work in an immersive, plant-filled environment and experience the physiological and psychological benefits plants provide. It's an idea that may sound simple, until you begin to think about what kind of environment allows for both the plants and the people to be comfortable and productive. If you've ever entered a tropical greenhouse on a summer day, you know that comfort is not the first word that comes to mind. Aware of the needs of both groups, the professionals created a perfectly balanced climate, one inspired by tropical cloud forests with higher humidity but moderate temperatures. People get priority in the daytime, with temperatures in the 68- to 72-degree F range and relative humidity at 60 percent. At night it's all about the plants, as temperatures decrease to 55 to 58 degrees F and humidity rises to 80 percent or more.

Within months of opening, Amazon implemented a public access program—a reservation system that allows the public to tour the Spheres for free the first and third Saturdays of each month. The atmosphere is casual, yet everywhere you look there are unusual plants, some quite rare, others common in some parts of the world, but not seen elsewhere in the Pacific Northwest. The facility provides an opportunity for employees and visitors to appreciate and learn about the plants around them. The Spheres are not a shopping mall–like environment where plants are cycled in and out every month—these plants live here. That said, every time you visit, you'll probably discover something new as plants grow, bloom, and interact differently with each other.

The Spheres project and the uncommon plants used throughout the Amazon campus have resulted in the assembly of a top-notch horticulture team to source, propagate, and care for these plants. Bringing vast experience and horticulture knowledge to their work are Ron Gagliardo, who heads up the horticulture team; Justin Schroeder, the Amazon Spheres program manager; and Michael Fong, who runs the off-site greenhouse. Local specialty nurseries like Far Reaches Farm, Keeping It Green Nursery, Cistus Nursery, and Dan Hinkley's Windcliff Plants made finding and acquiring special plants a little easier.

One of the most dramatic features of the Spheres, whether you're inside or out, is the 67-foot-high living wall. This vertical garden contains over 25,000 plants: ferns, bromeliads, anthuriums—there are even agaves! The wall uses a special mesh fabric in a system developed by Ben Eiben, Amazon's vertical horticultural manager. The wall itself is built of three-foot-square sections that were put together at Amazon's greenhouse in Redmond, Washington, then disassembled, moved, and reassembled on-site. Ben has an app on his phone that he uses to remotely monitor the wall's systems and health.

You may be tempted to think that gardening indoors, within a fixed climate, eliminates changing microclimates like we home gardeners have in our in-ground gardens. Not so. As construction

continues on the buildings around the Spheres, and as the angle of the sun changes with the seasons, the amount of sunlight reflecting off the glass on surrounding buildings changes. This reflected light causes hot spots that have actually burned plant leaves—a good lesson to remember for other urban gardeners who have plants near their windows.

The conservatories are used as alternative workspace, a temporary escape from traditional offices, meant to be used for meetings, brainstorming, or just relaxing. Because the spaces are no one's full-time office, it's only natural that the magic of being surrounded by plants while in these havens would transfer back to the desks around the Amazon campus. Claire Woodward, a member of the Sphere's horticulture crew, says the team makes themselves available to help employees with desk-plant selections and has a page on the internal website where they make plant suggestions "tailored to the light (office spaces vary from intense light by the window to those requiring additional light farthest from a window), temperature, and in particular the humidity found in the offices on campus." Employees email the team with questions about their own plants or plants they see at the Spheres or around campus. The team also has plans to host a desk-plant help desk at the farmers' markets that occur on the playfield next to the Spheres. After all, as Claire reminds us, an "ailing plant on a desk would not be a positive experience of biophilia!" Introduced by biologist Edward O. Wilson, the biophilia hypothesis states that we humans have an innate desire to connect with nature and other forms of life.

Outside the Spheres, the multi-block downtown Seattle Amazon campus feels like an urban arboretum, or maybe a neighborhood botanical garden that surrounds high-rise buildings where once there were just surface parking lots. As the campus expands to cover all four and a half blocks, there will be choice plants—not merely decorative, but evocative—on every block. One of the last blocks of the site is slated to feature plants native to Cascadia, the bioregion of Northern California, Oregon, Washington, and British Columbia.

Much has been said about the changes Amazon and its remarkable growth have brought to the Seattle area. Focusing on the horticultural angle, it's an amazing gift for visitors, city residents, and workers to have well-planted public spaces to enjoy. Not just default public plantings, but gardens pushing the limits of what an urban space can be. In creating these gardens, the team doing the work is raising the bar for what's considered the norm in urban corporate horticulture. Hopefully other developers in the area will rise to the standard Amazon has set.

GARDENING WISDOM FROM MATTHEW WOOD, PRINCIPAL AT SITE WORKSHOP, THE LANDSCAPE ARCHITECTURE FIRM ON THE AMAZON PROJECTS:

- Make it a priority to shop at smaller specialty nurseries. There are so many good plants that you won't find anywhere else—and yes, their prices are fair. That's what it actually costs to produce a high-quality plant, pay fair wages, and run a sustainable operation. These nurseries won't exist without your support.

- There's so much more to plants than just color, form, and texture. Be curious about culinary, medicinal, and other uses; ecological associations; conservation value; botany; all of it. Gardening isn't just exterior decorating; it's a vital connection to the natural world.

- A garden is a process, a relationship. It changes over time. Learn when to intervene and when to step back and let the garden's own internal dynamics play out—when in doubt, wait and see what happens. Err on the wild side.

- As our friend Ron Determann says, "All plants are epiphytes until proven otherwise." So, remember that roots need air, too. Most plants respond well to good drainage, especially around their crown. In the garden, that means protecting your soil from compaction; don't work it when it's wet, and skip any kind of tilling. Let your soil develop a natural structure that allows even clay soils to drain well—where winters are wet, some plants appreciate being planted on a mound, or even in a four- to six-inch layer of fine gravel.

Point Defiance Zoo & Aquarium

Zoo grounds within a public park, located in Tacoma, Washington. pdza.org

It took an email from Bryon Jones, lead horticulturist/arborist at the Point Defiance Zoo & Aquarium (PDZA), to get me to visit. He invited me for a tour, writing, "My passion is desert plants, I think we have that in common." Boy, he got that right!

A Pacific Northwest native, Bryon didn't catch the plant bug until he spent a year in the south of France, a region with a climate similar to that of San Diego, California. The beauty of the setting, and the diversity of plants grown there—he describes a Mediterranean wonderland where jungle and desert plants grow side by side—hooked him for life. Years later, Bryon finally got to design a garden around his home in Gig Harbor, Washington. He created a botanical mash-up that evoked a similar feeling of paradise, mixing big-leaf bananas, hardy palms, tall yuccas, and prickly pear cactus. That garden was a fantastic primer and testing ground for the horticultural magic he's been working at the PDZA since 2005.

At the zoo, Bryon says his personal mission is to educate on "the interconnectedness of people, plants, and animals." He and his staff build gardens that support the needs of the animals, while also striving to spark a little plant curiosity in the people who visit. To bring the curious into the fold a little further, Bryon leads monthly tours focused on different plants in the PDZA gardens and the stories those plants tell. Topics he's covered include a look at garden soils, to "get up close with the important stuff that grows our plants." Living fossils like ferns, conifers, cycads, and ginkgos have also received attention; there have been tours of the big leafy plants that provide a jungle feel in the Pacific Northwest; and of course, sometimes Bryon focuses on plants with thorns, spikes, and zigzagging stems.

Clockwise from top left:

The desert bed near the entry to the Point Defiance Zoo & Aquarium includes a pair of *Nolina nelsonii* with beefy trunks, and several *Agave parryi* var. *huachucensis*.

Aloiampelos striatula and *Opuntia ellisiana*, surrounded by *Othonna cheirifolia*, another desert bed vignette.

It may be from Chile, but this *Araucaria araucana* (monkey puzzle tree) thrives at PDZA.

An animal enclosure in the Asian Forest Sanctuary is densely planted with *Gunnera tinctoria*, *Ensete ventricosum* 'Maurelii', *Schefflera taiwaniana* 'Yuan Shan', and *Trachycarpus fortunei*.

Bryon calls the area next to the aquarium the Baja Bed; he designed the plantings to look as much like Mexico's Baja Peninsula as is possible in the Pacific Northwest. The pines are *Pinus contorta* var. *contorta* and the tall yucca is *Yucca rostrata*.

Also in the Baja Bed: *Pinus contorta* 'Spaan's Dwarf', *Yucca filamentosa*, and *Agave gentryi*.

Clockwise from top:

A forest of *Echium pininana* at the Point Defiance Zoo & Aquarium. This plant is not well known in the Pacific Northwest, as it's only marginally hardy here.

The silver spears of *Astelia chathamica, Melianthus major,* and *Nolina nelsonii,* under the canopy of an *Araucaria araucana.*

On the left is *Agave parryi* var. *huachucensis*; on the right, *Agave parryi* var. *truncata.*

Bryon hopes those who take part in the tours learn something new, or notice a small feature of a plant they hadn't before. One visitor was thrilled to learn that several varieties of lilies—*Lilium tigrinum,* for example—form tiny bulbils on their leaf axils, which fall to the ground and become new plants. Although it can take up to three years for the bulbils to become large enough to bloom, they eventually will.

Of course, the zoo animals are a huge draw for kids, but imagine letting them cut open the pitcher of a carnivorous plant, such as a sarracenia, and finding living (or not so living, anymore) proof that plants can eat animals. Just like that, another budding botanist might be born.

Visiting the PDZA is like walking through a botanical garden with multiple habitats. The different gardens support the illusion that you're actually in the place the animals are from, be it the arctic tundra or Mexico's Baja Peninsula. Returning to his mission statement, Bryon stresses, "The landscapes are about sharing stories of ecosystems, how plants and animals connect." Visitors walk through plantings that represent native Northwest vegetation, and then on to a desert garden, and later an Asian forest sanctuary. The Red Wolf Woods exhibit contains plants from the southeastern United States, where red wolves are native. Having all these different environments in one setting provides gardeners with inspiration for whatever type of garden they may want to grow. That is another of Bryon's principles: "Grow what you want, garden how you want to garden!"

From picked flowers to trampled plants (when paths are created where none previously existed), gardening in the public realm can be challenging. At a zoo, though, you also have animals "stomping, picking, and chewing" on the plants around them. Bryon has a small staff—two other full-time gardeners and some seasonal help—to care for the plants in the 29-acre facility. That seems like a daunting task, but somehow they manage to make it look effortless. I doubt Bryon planned the drought-tolerant desert planting near the entrance to act as a time-saver, but the easygoing and resilient plants save on both staff maintenance time and water usage. Plus, it gets visitors asking, "Can you really grow that here?"

Bryon points to an agave in the desert bed to illustrate the importance he places on trying something several times before you declare that you can't grow it. Sometimes it's the seventh, eighth, or ninth try that works. It took him 12 years to find just the right spot for an *Agave parryi* var. *truncata* to take hold. That's an extraordinary level of persistence. Bryon recommends planting multiples of a plant whenever you can, testing different combinations of soil, air, and light conditions. "If you can afford it, don't be afraid to try things out. Research and make an educated choice," he says. In his previous home garden, he planted two clumps of *Musa basjoo* (hardy banana). One clump grew to 10 feet tall, the other over 27 feet. He determined the only difference was the lesser amount of sun the shorter clump received. Moving it just 10 feet increased the amount of sun and the banana responded by growing taller.

Climate-wise, the zoo gardens enjoy the benefit of sitting right at the south end of Western Washington's Puget Sound, on a protected peninsula with a warm microclimate. Still, winter weather can test the plants. February 2019 brought an unofficial low of 18 degrees F and about 10 inches of wet snow that hung around for days. Several years back there was a three-week period with overnight temperatures in the teens and low twenties F. Bryon reports the weather on the point is mild in general, but the topography can trap weather systems and dump moisture that isn't falling in other parts of town. When it comes to winter protection, the PDZA gardeners don't have time for elaborate methods. Mulching *Musa basjoo* and *Melianthus major* with their own leaves is about the extent of it. Asked if he met any resistance from zoo officials when it came to planting out the spiky desert bed Bryon said no—their only reaction was that they didn't think the plants would live, but figured there was no harm in trying. Exactly!

BRYON'S INSIGHTS ABOUT FEARLESS GARDENING:

- Everyone wants to tell you how to garden, but you've got to decide for yourself what success is.

- Gardening is both science and art. The science part is understanding the plants' cultural needs, the art is how you combine the plants. There's nothing difficult about gardening; success is in the details of planting and maintaining.

- Try new things, take the time to investigate where plants come from (their natural habitat), and learn from that. Visit gardens in your area and talk to people.

- Gardening is great for mental health and an enjoyable way to connect with nature. Take time to feel, smell, and notice amazing small details of plants.

- Have fun with gardening. Envision designing and artfully arranging plants for a picture or painting.

Point Defiance Zoo & Aquarium

danger garden

My private garden, located in Portland, Oregon. thedangergarden.com

I used to bristle at the idea that my garden needed a name or that it was, by default, danger garden. *Danger garden* is a blog, and my garden is my garden. The blog name was my husband's (genius) suggestion, based on the fact I had several spiky plants and we had recently adopted a small dog we named Lila—a Chihuahua-pug mix with big eyes. Eventually, when a group came through on tour and two people ended up bleeding profusely from agave puncture wounds, I had to admit the name fit. And so it is: danger garden (lower case intentional, so as not to be too threatening).

Spikes and glochids, sword-shaped leaves with sharp tips, carnivorous and poisonous plants: these are elements of danger. Unlike a friend who set out to create the macabre—she has an area she named the Ruby Red Death Bed—my garden is simply made up of plants I love, not intentionally dangerous ones. I'm also a plant collector. When I asked Riz Reyes about his personal garden style, he called himself an aesthetic hoarder—a plant hoarder with a design sense. I can relate. While I want all the cool plants, I also want a beautiful garden. The two are often mutually exclusive, but I like to think I've created a balance.

My family moved into our current house and garden in the summer of 2005. We had big plans but didn't start chipping away at the inherited weedy lawn until the next spring. The front garden was the first to go in, a tropicalesque design that grew fast and looked fabulous. It was filled with phormiums, cordylines, canna lilies, and big grasses—until back-to-back harsh winters and dead plants had me rethinking my approach. I decided to take the majority of my zone pushing to the back garden and play it a little safer out front, sparing the neighbors a scorched-earth style

Clockwise from top left:

My front garden in September—it gets by with just a few deep soakings over our hot, dry, summers.

The shrub with the graceful dark branching is *Arctostaphylos* × 'Austin Griffiths'.

The shady side of the upper, back garden is next to the garage. The seasonal bromeliad additions seem to grow in number and size every year.

Clockwise from top left:

Entering the back garden, where by August the plants are threatening to engulf the pathway.

Looking toward the patio and our outdoor dining area. The patio is a little more than a foot lower than the rest of the back garden.

Looking back toward the garage and the upper garden. Readers of my blog may recognize Sammy, the tall *Yucca rostrata* 'Sapphire Skies', and Clifford, the bigleaf *Magnolia macrophylla*. Sometimes plants have so much character, they simply must be named.

The shade pavilion backs up to the south side of our property.

New plants can always find a home in a container.

The upper garden is a favorite space, where I can sit surrounded by plants.

garden every winter, but still planting the unexpected—a zonal denial garden.

I started over, replanting with unusual things I'd been watching in other gardens, things that had survived the cold and looked great year round. The new plantings managed to fulfill my vision of what my garden should be—things like hardy opuntias from a neighbor, *Yucca rostrata*, *Dasylirion wheeleri*, *Arctostaphylos* × 'Austin Griffiths', and plenty of agaves. These plants provide structure and allow for small experiments to play out between them. Like *Echium wildpretii* that may or may not overwinter. Or a windfall of mangaves—hybrids between the genera *Manfreda* and *Agave*—from a plant breeder, plants of unproven hardiness that I was willing to try out to see how they would perform.

I treat the front garden as an all-season space. Sure, there are more flowers in summer, fallen leaves in autumn, and a few perennials napping underground in the winter, but there's always something interesting happening. It also intentionally has low water needs, getting by on just a few deep soaks over our long, dry summers. Some people feel it's a little crunchy, but I love testing just how far I can push the xeric planting style.

Since the house sits toward the front of our 45-by-111-foot lot, the back garden is a little deeper than you expect and even includes an elevation change. A large rectangle at the back of the property is just over a foot lower than the rest of the garden. All lawn when we moved in, this sunken spot provided the perfect location for a private patio surrounded on two sides by a retaining wall—a natural perch for small potted plants.

After years of planting, I now sit in the back garden completely surrounded by plants, enveloped in a jungle of my creation—it's a wonderful feeling. While I didn't intentionally design the space with rooms (that's what houses are for), it naturally evolved to have three distinct spaces. The upper garden, closest to the house, still has a bit of lawn. I keep it for the calming, cooling feel it brings to the space. As a lover of going barefoot in the summertime, it's soft on my feet, but there's a cement-paver pathway through the grass for use during the wet season. A chair in the lawn provides a place to soak up the evening sun after the patio area has gone completely shady, thanks to the tall trees in our neighbor's yard to the west.

The patio, or second room, is the perfect place for my containerized plant collection, as well as our dining table and chairs. The walk from the house to the back of the property allows the patio to feel like a destination, removed from the house and indoor life.

Behind our garage is the shade pavilion, called such because its original purpose was to provide a shady spot, relief from the hot and sunny patio. Now it pulls double duty and provides winter protection as a greenhouse that keeps some of those container plants dry and warm when it's cold outside.

I don't think the garden would feel as relaxing as it does without the structure provided by the paver path through the lawn, the concrete brick lawn edging, the large patio, the retaining wall, and the gravel and paver area by the shade pavilion. The hardscape truly does contain the plant chaos and create a sense of order.

I look around my garden and marvel at the plants surrounding me. Of course, in high summer, after months of adding non-hardy container plants bought at local nurseries and plant sales, I also wonder where I'm going to put them all come winter. My collection of bromeliads and succulents continues to grow. Ultimately though, it's a good problem to have.

The contrasts in color and foliage texture between *Agave ovatifolia* 'Frosty Blue', *Daphne ×houtteana,* and *Amsonia hubrichtii* become even more dramatic when the amsonia takes on its golden fall color.

I remember having thoughts, early on in the process, along the lines of, "When the garden is done . . ." I know now that I will never be done with the garden. As soon as I have a little extra time, there's a bit of lawn to remove in a spot that's become too shady for it to grow well. I need to dig it out and replant the area with some low-growing shade lovers (new plants!). I keep meaning to install drip irrigation in a few moisture-loving spots, and editing continues. There are so many more plants I want to grow, I must make space for them and keep experimenting.

Much of what
I've learned
in my garden
adventures over
the years has
been shared
throughout
the pages of
this book, but
I will leave you
with these final
takeaways:

- Not everyone is going to like what you create, and that's okay. Garden for yourself.

- Gardening is not a straight line and you never actually arrive at the finish. These truths apply to the act of building a garden, but also to the practice of gardening. Rarely does a day spent in the garden unfold exactly as planned. That's a good thing. Enjoy the detours.

- Years ago, I heard a well-known garden writer say something along the lines of, "My garden is just the place I keep my plants" when explaining that the way her garden looked wasn't something she spent much time thinking about. While I laughed at the time, this strikes me as such a sad statement. Your garden can be so much more than just the place you keep your plants.

- When explaining to friends—mainly non-gardeners—what fearless gardening means, I find myself referring to the slogan used by *that* Oregon athletic shoe company. You know the one: "Just do it." There are many roadblocks between you and the garden of your dreams— some real, some imagined. But you'll never get there if you don't get started. So just do it.

- I'll say it one last time: experiment, play, kill plants. Being brave is integral to gardening fearlessly. Do all these things—frequently, deliberately, passionately.

METRIC CONVERSIONS

INCHES	CENTIMETERS
1	2.5
2	5.0
5	12.7

FEET	METERS
1	0.3
2	0.6
3	0.9
4	1.2
5	1.5
10	3.0
50	15.2
100	30.5

FURTHER READING & RESOURCES

WEBSITES AND BLOGS

The Amazon Spheres: seattlespheres.com

danger garden: thedangergarden.com

The Frustrated Gardener: frustratedgardener.com

The Garden Conservancy: gardenconservancy.org

Hillside Desert Botanical Gardens: hdbgi.com

Keeyla Meadows: keeylameadows.net

Lotusland: lotusland.org

McMenamins: mcmenamins.com

Missouri Botanical Garden: missouribotanicalgarden.org

The Outlaw Gardener: outlawgarden.blogspot.com

Paintbrush Gardens: paintbrushgardens.com

The Pearl Fryar Topiary Garden: gardenconservancy.org/
    preservation/pearl-fryar

Plant Lust: plantlust.com

The Planthunter: theplanthunter.com.au

Point Defiance Zoo & Aquarium: pdza.org

The Ruth Bancroft Garden: ruthbancroftgarden.org

San Marcos Growers: smgrowers.com

USDA Plant Hardiness Zone Map: planthardiness.ars.usda.gov

BOOKS

Bonine, Paul, and Amy Campion. 2017. *Gardening in the Pacific Northwest: The Complete Homeowner's Guide.* Portland, OR: Timber Press.

Crawford, Sharon. 1996. *Ganna Walska Lotusland: The Garden and its Creators.* Santa Barbara, CA: Companion Press.

Francko, David A. 2003. *Palms Won't Grow Here and Other Myths: Warm-Climate Plants for Cooler Areas.* Portland, OR: Timber Press.

Keys, Andrew. 2012. *Why Grow That When You Can Grow This?: 255 Extraordinary Alternatives to Everyday Problem Plants.* Portland, OR: Timber Press.

Meadows, Keeyla. 2009. *Fearless Color Gardens: The Creative Gardener's Guide to Jumping Off the Color Wheel.* Portland, OR: Timber Press.

Schenk, George. 2006. *Gardening on Pavement, Tables, and Hard Surfaces.* Portland, OR: Timber Press.

Silver, Johanna. 2016. *The Bold Dry Garden: Lessons from the Ruth Bancroft Garden.* Portland, OR: Timber Press.

Soler, Ivette. 2011. *The Edible Front Yard: The Mow-Less, Grow-More Plan for a Beautiful, Bountiful Garden.* Portland, OR: Timber Press.

Thomas, R. William. 2015. *The Art of Gardening: Design Inspiration and Innovative Planting Techniques from Chanticleer.* Portland, OR: Timber Press.

Tychonievich, Joseph. 2016. *Rock Gardening: Reimagining a Classic Style.* Portland, OR: Timber Press.

NURSERIES
I RECOMMEND

MAIL-ORDER NURSERIES

Annie's Annuals & Perennials: anniesannuals.com

Bird Rock Tropicals: birdrocktropicals.com

Cistus Nursery: cistus.com

The Desert Northwest: desertnorthwest.com

Far Reaches Farm: farreachesfarm.com

Gossler Farms Nursery: gosslerfarms.com

Grassy Knoll Exotic Plants: gkplants.com

Joy Creek Nursery: joycreek.com

Keeping It Green Nursery: keepingitgreennursery.com

Little Prince of Oregon Nursery: littleprinceoforegonnursery.com

Rhododendron Species Botanical Garden: rhodygarden.org

Sarracenia Northwest: growcarnivorousplants.com

Sebright Gardens: sebrightgardens.com

Secret Garden Growers: secretgardengrowers.com

Rare Plant Research: rareplantresearch.com

PORTLAND-AREA NURSERIES & PLANT SHOPS

If you find yourself in the Portland area, here are a few local, non–mail order nurseries where I've bought a lot of plants over the years:

Cornell Farm: cornellfarms.com

Garden Fever: gardenfever.com

Pomarius: pomariusnursery.com

Portland Nursery: portlandnursery.com

Xera Plants: xeraplants.com

GARDENS TO VISIT

(**P**) Indicates private gardens
that are sometimes open for tours.
All others are open to the public.

WASHINGTON

The Amazon Spheres, Seattle (**P**)

Kubota Garden, Seattle

Pacific Connections Garden and the Washington
   Park Arboretum, Seattle

Bellevue Botanical Garden, Bellevue

Rhododendron Species Botanical Garden, Federal Way

Point Defiance Zoo & Aquarium, Tacoma

Hillside Desert Botanical Gardens, Yakima (**P**)

Manito Park and Botanical Gardens, Spokane

OREGON

Elk Rock Gardens of the Bishop's Close, Portland

Hoyt Arboretum, Portland

Lan Su Chinese Garden, Portland

Leach Botanical Garden, Portland

Portland Japanese Garden, Portland

Rogerson Clematis Garden, West Linn

CALIFORNIA

Ruth Bancroft Garden, Walnut Creek

University of California Botanical Garden at Berkeley, Berkeley

San Francisco Botanical Garden at Strybing Arboretum, San Francisco

Lotusland, Montecito (**P**)

Santa Barbara Botanic Garden, Santa Barbara

Taft Botanic Gardens and Nature Preserve, Ojai (**P**)

Huntington Botanical Gardens, San Marino

Los Angeles County Arboretum and Botanic Garden, Arcadia

Pitzer College Campus, Claremont

California Botanic Garden, Claremont

Balboa Park, San Diego

San Diego Botanic Garden, Encinitas

ARIZONA

Desert Botanical Garden, Phoenix

Boyce Thompson Arboretum, Superior

Arizona-Sonora Desert Museum, Tucson

Tucson Botanical Garden, Tucson

ACKNOWLEDGMENTS

Becoming a gardener is not something you do on your own, and neither is writing a book. I am deeply indebted to the people who opened their gardens and shared their time and plant passions with me. You inspire me.

Before these pages were sent off to the publisher, several generous individuals took the time to read through and make suggestions on improvements. Andrew Bohl, Patricia Cunningham, Bill Wagenblatt, Gerhard Bock, and Lorene Edwards Forkner—thank you.

It seems obvious, but any errors or omissions of credit are mine and mine alone. I've done my best to make sure there are none, but I know enough to realize they will happen. I can only hope they aren't too substantial.

Thank you to my wonderful husband, Andrew Bohl, who encouraged me to take on this project and has supported my garden and plant passions all these years. Thank you to my parents, Phyllis and John Moore, lifelong gardeners who shared their love of gardening with me, ensuring that it would become an important part of my life.

Finally, thank you to my fellow plant people. To the nursery women and men who work hard to make exciting and healthy plants available, and to the many gardeners willing to share their gardens and hard-earned knowledge. Gardeners really are the very best people.

PHOTOGRAPHY CREDITS

All photographs are by the author, except the following:

Alison Conliffe, page 65, bottom right

J. R. Eyerman, page 23

Peter Herpst, page 65, top right

Saxon Holt, page 18

Anna Kullgren, page 185, top left

Marianne Majerus, pages 115 all; 117

Kenton J. Seth, page 96

Richie Steffen, page 183, top

Claire Woods, page 142

INDEX

Gerhard Bock

ABOUT
THE AUTHOR

Loree's popular blog and website, thedangergarden.com, launched in 2009, and she quickly found her tribe. Not only did she connect with gardeners in sunny, warm places like Los Angeles, Albuquerque, and Austin, she also discovered a network of nearby spiky-plant enthusiasts.

In addition to freelance garden writing and scouting assignments, as well as speaking engagements, Loree has served on the boards of directors for the Hardy Plant Society of Oregon, the Pacific Horticulture Society, and the Garden Bloggers Fling Advisory Committee. Garden travel is high on her list of leisure pursuits as she enjoys seeing other regional gardening styles, how climates influence gardeners' plant choices, and how those plants are grown. She practices the fine art of garden cramscaping and is a firm believer that there is always room for one more plant.

A lifelong resident of the Pacific Northwest, Loree and her husband Andrew moved to Portland in 2004. Having fallen in love with the city's vibrant horticultural community—even though warmer, drier, climates still call—she's firmly planted there and may never leave.